Welcome

Previous editions in the *Modelling British Railways* series have explored the world of engineers' wagons under British Rail ownership, the two volumes covering developments through to the mid-1990s and the privatisation of the network. This new volume picks up where these left off to bring the story right up to date and detail the best part of three decades of change.

As might be expected, the BR wagons did not disappear overnight, it took a number of years to replace the ageing vacuum-braked survivors and longer still to see off the air-braked fleet with high capacity replacements. Even today in 2023, this process is not yet finished, although the end is finally in sight for the venerable Salmon rail and track carriers. Having already expended two magazines on the BR fleet, these are not covered in the same level of detail as before, but all the major developments are explained alongside a selection of models.

Instead, much of this volume is given over to the many types of ballast, sleeper and rail wagons that have appeared since the mid-1990s, be they conversions or new builds. Under the three shadow privatisation freight companies and then EWS, rebodying existing chassis was very much in vogue and the last stragglers of this policy can still be observed today, albeit in ever decreasing numbers.

This century has seen Network Rail and the various freight companies prefer to go for new designs, these offering considerable increases in payload while the use of automation and, more recently, modular designs are modern traits. New methods of operation have also appeared as technology has developed, leading to the introduction of dedicated trains for particular duties. Undoubtedly the best known of these are the autumnal Railhead Treatment Trains and their 20 year history is detailed in full.

Modelling this period has been greatly aided over the years by the ready-to-run manufacturers, the already decent number of models having swelled considerably in recent times thanks to the appearance of the plethora of new companies. While there are still gaps, including some significant ones, there is plenty that can be recreated in miniature and such projects feature throughout these pages alongside details of what is available from the trade.

As is customary, thanks are due to the various people who have contributed towards this publication, including David Ratcliffe for his ever invaluable notes on wagon histories and operations. On the modelling front, the input of Terry Bendall, Mick Bryan, Mike Cubberley, Timara Easter, and James Makin has been equally essential along with that of the photographers named throughout.

Simon Bendall
Editor

ABOVE: Ballast trains have come a long way in the privatisation era with the creation of virtual quarry stockpiles at strategic locations across the country an early policy of Railtrack that is continued today by its successor Network Rail. With these requiring constant resupply, the transport of bulk ballast has become a significant traffic for the freight operators. The quarry at Mountsorrel has long been a key supplier of ballast and on April 29, 2013, Freightliner's 70013 powers along at Barrow upon Trent with 6U77, this conveying another load of Leicestershire stone to Crewe Basford Hall. The uniform rake of 23 IOA boxes is entirely typical for the train, the wagons doing the work for which they were built. Timara Easter

COVER: Network Rail's autoballaster hoppers have become one of the most common and recognisable wagon fleets over the past two decades. On March 24, 2019, 56105 and 56096 top and tail a set of HQAs at Althorp while working the 6C30 12.00 Kilburn Up and Down Loop to Crewe Basford Hall empties. Dave Smith

Modelling BR: Engineers Wagons of Privatisation **3**

HORNBY® 2023 CATALOGUE

The eagerly awaited *2023 Hornby Catalogue* is here, detailing all the maker's key model rail releases for the next 12 months together with detailed information on existing favourites. Full of hundreds of exciting new releases across various categories, the *2023 Hornby Catalogue* is set to be a winner!

Whether you're purchasing it to add to your collection, you're new to the hobby and looking for informative and useful reading material, or you're after a gift for a model railway enthusiast, the *2023 Hornby Catalogue* ticks all the boxes! **228pp**

ONLY £10.99
PLUS FREE P&P*
*Free 2nd class P&P on all UK & BFPO orders. Overseas charges apply.

ORDER DIRECT
ALSO AVAILABLE FROM WHSmith AND ALL LEADING NEWSAGENTS

HORNBY MAGAZINE SUBSCRIBERS CALL FOR YOUR £4 DISCOUNT!

Free P&P* when you order online at
shop.keypublishing.com/hornbycat23

OR

Call UK: **01780 480404**
Overseas: **+44 1780 480404**

IF YOU ARE INTERESTED IN THE 2023 HORNBY CATALOGUE, YOU MAY ALSO LIKE...

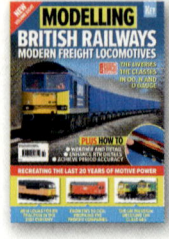 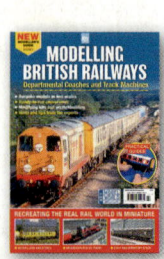  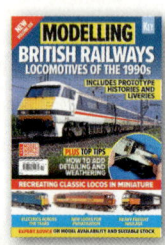  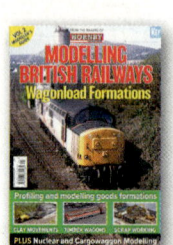 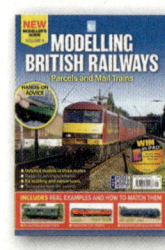

Contents

ABOVE: On-track plant has become increasingly significant throughout the privatisation era with mechanisation designed to speed many processes previously conducted manually. Disappointingly, this has yet to be recognised in model form to any great extent with most of the colourful fleets of track machines unavailable. One exception is Bachmann's outstanding recreation of the Multi-Purpose Vehicles employed by Network Rail for sandite, de-icing, weedkilling and other roles. The OO gauge model has recently returned to the manufacturer's range after a long absence in new South West Trains colour schemes, but this is one of the original releases pictured on George Woodcock's layout of Georgemas Junction when still owned by Railtrack. DR98905 and DR98965 have been converted to weedkilling format using the short-lived and long discontinued resin modules once produced by SJR Models. *Dennis Taylor*

6 A change of ownership	**62** High capacity upgrades
8 British Rail survivors	**90** A modular future
32 Railtrack renewal	**108** The war on leaves

ISBN 978 1 80282 751 4
Editor: Simon Bendall
Main contributors: James Makin, David Ratcliffe
Senior editor, specials: Roger Mortimer
Email: roger.mortimer@keypublishing.com
Cover design: Dan Jarman
Design: SJmagic DESIGN SERVICES, India
Advertising Sales Manager: Brodie Baxter
Email: brodie.baxter@keypublishing.com
Tel: 01780 755131
Advertising Production: Debi McGowan
Email: debi.mcgowan@keypublishing.com

SUBSCRIPTION/MAIL ORDER
Key Publishing Ltd, PO Box 300, Stamford, Lincs, PE9 1NA
Tel: 01780 480404
Subscriptions email: subs@keypublishing.com

Mail Order email: orders@keypublishing.com
Website: www.keypublishing.com/shop

PUBLISHING
Group CEO: Adrian Cox
Publisher, Books and Bookazines: Jonathan Jackson
Published by
Key Publishing Ltd, PO Box 100, Stamford, Lincs, PE9 1XQ
Tel: 01780 755131 **Website:** www.keypublishing.com

PRINTING
Precision Colour Printing Ltd, Haldane, Halesfield 1, Telford, Shropshire. TF7 4QQ

DISTRIBUTION
Seymour Distribution Ltd, 2 Poultry Avenue, London, EC1A 9PU
Enquiries Line: 02074 294000.

We are unable to guarantee the bonafides of any of our advertisers. Readers are strongly recommended to take their own precautions before parting with any information or item of value, including, but not limited to money, manuscripts, photographs, or personal information in response to any advertisements within this publication.

© Key Publishing Ltd 2023
All rights reserved. No part of this magazine may be reproduced or transmitted in any form by any means, electronic or mechanical, including photocopying, recording or by any information storage and retrieval system, without prior permission in writing from the copyright owner. Multiple copying of the contents of the magazine without prior written approval is not permitted.

Modelling BR: Engineers Wagons of Privatisation **5**

A change of ownership

With the arrival of privatisation, there was a change in ownership for the wagons making up the BR engineers' fleet, most of these passing through the regional freight companies to EWS and later DB. Subsequently, Railtrack and Network Rail acquired wagons of their own and leased yet more while other freight operators also became involved. Simon Bendall looks at how operations have altered since 1994.

As British Rail was readied for the privatisation process to begin in early 1994, the effects of the restructuring were felt by the engineers' fleet. The previous two years had seen most infrastructure rolling stock come under the control of the three passenger sectors of InterCity, Network SouthEast, and Regional Railways, these owning both the locomotives and wagons as well as being responsible for their upkeep. Money was tight, especially on the wagon side, and what new conversions were authorised sometimes did not have enough in the budget to even pay for a full repaint.

March 1994 saw the infrastructure side of things split away from the passenger sectors and placed back in the control of the freight operators. A much more logical fit, this month brought the abolition of the Trainload Freight sub-sectors in favour of the three regional freight companies, which would go on to become Transrail, Loadhaul and Mainline Freight. These not only saw the loco fleet split between them but also virtually all of the wagons as well. This was, like the motive power, largely done by the existing allocations so types that were concentrated in certain parts of the country stayed where they were.

It was not long before this new ownership came to be displayed on the wagons, although the style of brandings varied considerably. Reflecting the original names of the new freight companies, 'TLF-W' and 'TLF South East' or similar became common, being shorthand for Trainload Freight West and Trainload Freight South East. Once the firms had selected their new names, such simple brandings gave way to Transrail's 'T' logo, usually in white or occasionally colour, while Mainline wording on a dark blue background was widespread. Loadhaul tended not to brand its wagons with its logo although some derivations of TLF North East did appear early on.

The new liveries of the freight companies duly followed on from the logos, featuring most prominently on wagons fresh from conversion, such as ZCA Sea Urchins, or those newly overhauled. Transrail opted to employ light grey, sometimes with red added, while Mainline used its attractive dark blue scheme, normally with yellow relief. Loadhaul went with its bold black and orange, offset with a hint of white, with the application style varying depending on what wagon type was involved. Some wagon fleets saw more repaints than others, such as Sealion and Seacow ballast hoppers along with Shark ballast ploughs, but the three companies were not in existence for long enough for any of the liveries to find widespread use.

EWS reunification

With Wisconsin Central acquiring all three regional freight companies in February 1996, they were soon reunited under the EWS banner, once again bringing unified control of the engineers' wagon fleet. As with the company's locos, maroon repaints were soon underway on newly overhauled wagons, Seacows again being a primary recipient along with accompanying Shark plough vans, the latter being less standardised in how they were repainted.

Given the short life expectancy of much of the inherited ex-BR fleet, maroon and gold was not often applied to other engineers' types but there was the odd exception. Instead, there was a limited branding exercise with EWS lettering appearing in various styles and sometimes on a maroon patch. Full EWS colours became more widespread as it put various conversion programmes in place, firstly with more Sea Urchins appearing

ABOVE: The look of engineers' services in the mid to late 1990s is encapsulated by this view of 37114 *City of Worcester* rumbling past the container terminal at Millbrook, Southampton, on April 15, 1997, with an unidentified working, most likely from Eastleigh. While the Type 3 is relatively fresh in maroon and gold with original EW&S lettering, all but one of the wagons are still finished in their BR colours, these being ZFA Gunnells, YGB/YGH Seacow/Sealions and OAA/ZDA opens. Only one of the Gunnells stands out in Mainline Freight blue, a mere handful of the former PGA hoppers receiving such a repaint. This is likely one of DC390642 or DC390645, which had blue upper bodywork, while DC390560 retained the broad expanse of yellow. Martin Loader

A change of ownership

ABOVE: The construction of the Channel Tunnel Rail Link, later to become High Speed 1, was a significant undertaking at the beginning of this century. By September 2002, tracklaying was well underway from the line's construction base at Beechbrook Farm, on the outskirts of Ashford. This employed both Freightliner and GB Railfreight traction with a nearly new 66712 seen heading a rake of 23 HQA autoballasters alongside the temporary railhead. The Railtrack wagons were equally newly delivered, this being just a month before the national operator was replaced. *Simon Bendall*

and then the Coalfish in all their various derivatives. Equally, the appearance of the cut down MCA and MDA ballast opens and the follow on orders for the closely related MOA and MLA has ensured maroon is still widely seen in infrastructure workings today, or faded pink as it has become in some cases.

As EWS' successor, DB's principal contribution to the image of engineering trains has been the unmissable MXA Lobsters, their all-over red ensuring they stand out from a distance. Otherwise, the company has been largely uninterested in repainting the rest of its fleet, preferring to paint out or remove EWS brandings and sometimes apply DB replacements

Green to yellow

With little in the way of competition, EWS was Railtrack's primary supplier of traction and rolling stock through to the end of the 1990s. However, the infrastructure owner was acutely aware of the limitations of the wagons available to it, the creation of the virtual quarries driving the initial investment in new box wagon fleets. The PNA conversions and JNA new-builds not only brought the striking Railtrack emerald green livery to the network, but also the involvement of the wagon leasing companies, these two fleets initially being owned by Caib.

Railtrack again opted to lease, at least initially, when it plumped for the JJA autoballasters as the first key component of its revamped renewals fleet, striking a deal with GE Rail Services as it owned the aggregate hoppers employed as the basis of the conversions. However, Railtrack chose to be the outright owner when it came to the MRA side-tippers, these receiving the same beige livery with blue stripe as given to the autoballasters.

With Network Rail replacing Railtrack from 2002, its policy for a long time was to own rather than lease its wagon assets. Coinciding with this was the introduction of a new yellow livery when further autoballasters and MRAs were ordered in addition to the JNA Falcon ballast opens and IOA boxes for virtual quarry traffic. The yellow was subsequently retained for further wagon orders and has become Network Rail's default colour, much like grey and yellow was for British Rail during the 1980s and early 1990s.

Sharing the work

The over-reliance on EWS as traction provider for infrastructure traffic began to be loosened from 2000 as Freightliner's newly formed Heavy Haul division gained its first contract from Railtrack as part of the modernisation of the West Coast Main Line. GB Railfreight similarly won its first infrastructure contract the following year to launch its operations and both freight companies have remained involved in engineers traffic ever since.

It was GB Railfreight's contract with Metronet in 2006 that significantly increased its presence in the track renewals arena, the various wagon fleets acquired to support the upgrading of parts of the London Underground system still serving today out on the wider network. For a time in the late 2000s, Jarvis was a major sub-contractor to Network Rail with its track machine fleet and, as far as this publication is concerned, the Slinger track recovery trains. However, the company's collapse in 2010 largely took these wagon sets out of traffic for good.

Colas Rail is another freight company that owes its early growth to Network Rail haulage contracts, these initially covering work in the south of England, but which today have expanded to much of the country. In contrast, infrastructure work has largely been a profitable side-line for Direct Rail Services alongside its core nuclear and intermodal traffic but has again brought the company's traction to numerous parts of the company, particularly eastern England, the northwest, and Scotland.

For its most recent fleet renewal programme, Network Rail has returned to leasing wagons, a decision no doubt driven by its ever tightening budget. This has brought a new name to the UK scene in Wascosa, the European leasing firm partnering with GBRf to operate and maintain the 570-strong fleet until at least the end of the decade. While the fleet may be boldly branded with the name of their owner, they are, inevitably, still yellow!

ABOVE: Network Rail's infrastructure yards are now a sea of yellow as typified by Eastleigh East Yard on March 22, 2022. On this occasion, Railway Support Services-owned 08683 was propelling a rake of JNA Falcons and MLA into the yard following loading with fresh ballast at the virtual quarry on the opposite side of the station, while alongside a brand new rake of Wascosa-owned MLAs had been delivered that morning from Dollands Moor by 66720. With DB having withdrawn its last remaining shunters in December 2016, yard pilots are now provided by RSS at several GBRf-operated locations. *Stephen Stubbs*

Modelling BR: Engineers Wagons of Privatisation 7

British Rail survivors

British Rail survivors

From March 1994, large quantities of both air and vacuum-braked BR wagons passed to the regional freight companies and then onto EWS two years later. **Simon Bendall** looks at the trends that developed during this period.

ABOVE: Only the Transrail branding on 37197 gives the game away that this image is from the mid-1990s rather than the British Rail era a few years earlier. Now in EWS ownership, 37254 nosily leads its sister away from the Severn Tunnel at Pilning with the 7C40 12.06 Newport Alexandra Dock Junction to Exeter on October 2, 1996. In tow are two Shark ballast ploughs and a long string of ZFV Dogfish, all still displaying their BR colours. The Dogfish were the longest lived of the small BR ballast hoppers with those retaining vacuum brakes removed from traffic during 2001. Vacuum-braked Dogfish are available from Dapol in 2mm and Heljan in both 4mm and 7mm, Cambrian also offering its venerable 4mm kit. Martin Loader

The early 1990s brought some investment in new rolling stock for civil engineering duties, although as this was the perennially cash-strapped British Rail, new in this case amounted to buying second-hand fleets from the private sector and continuing the long tradition of repurposing good condition underframes by adding new bodywork. This had resulted in the creation of the ZFA Gunnell and ZKA Limpet fleets in the first instance and the emergence of the first ZCA Sea Urchin builds, allowing inroads to be made into the more elderly existing designs, such as the Grampus.

However, when the regional freight companies took over in the spring of 1994, they were still handed ownership of several thousand vacuum-braked wagons alongside the more recent air-braked types. With vacuum-braked stock already largely eliminated from commercial freight flows, its time was also coming to an end in engineers' use with both Transrail and Mainline Freight investing in further Sea Urchin conversions.

Loadhaul on the other hand preferred the less expensive option of overhauling SPA steel plate opens and sealing their doors shut to create additional ZCA Sea Hares. The northeast operator was also the only one of the trio to conduct the refurbishment of Dogfish ballast hoppers, the work seeing the vacuum brakes replaced by air with the resultant wagons recoded from ZFV to HPA.

Air only
However, it was under EWS ownership that the drive to oust vacuum-braked stock really accelerated. This was in part due to their age, high maintenance costs and low capacity but also spurred on by an operational need as the Class 66s arrived en masse between 1998 and 2000 to largely replace the inherited fleet of BR-built locos. Like the Class 56s, 58s, and 60s, the General Motors locos were incompatible with vacuum-braked stock, so the latter was targeted for mass replacement by means of further rebodies and new builds. Some vacuum-braked wagons did survive into the new century, such as the ZCV Clams now recoded as MGVs, but these soon faded away with the remaining Class 37s.

One avenue explored by the regional freight companies for a time, particularly by Mainline, and then EWS was to deploy former aggregates and scrap carrying JNA, JRA, JXA, and KEA bogie boxes on possession work, the theory being that these large wagons with capacities of between 68 and 75 tonnes could hold far more than existing engineers types. However, their high sides made them difficult to load on site while much more seriously, they were prone to being overloaded with sodden ballast and spoil.

As a result, axleloads were often far in excess of permitted limits and contributed to a series of incidents, including the spectacularly destructive derailment at Bexley in February 1997 when seven such wagons derailed and overturned, demolishing a section of arched viaduct and the industrial units located beneath with 500 tonnes of spoil spilling out. Thereafter, the use of such big boxes was restricted solely to virtual quarry deliveries where the loading was conducted in controlled conditions.

Departmental no more
Another policy implemented by EWS was to return wagons in departmental stock to their original TOPS codes if they were physically

British Rail survivors

unaltered as the company now viewed all of its rolling stock as revenue earning. This mostly affected the fleets of air-braked open wagons where ZDA Squid were re-coded back to OAA while ZDA Bass returned to OBA and OCA. The short-wheelbase ODA fleet also reappeared, having spent several years as ZDAs. Interestingly, official EWS literature from 1996 has these as assigned the codename of Roach, although there is no record of this being physically applied to any of the fleet.

The recoding policy also affected the bogie bolster fleets with many YAA Brill returning to their previous BDA designation while YNAs again became BPA Boplates. The SPA plate fleet was also strengthened by the reclassification of numerous ZAA Pike, while runner wagons for overhanging loads, such as the ZEA Bream, became RRA. Typically, the physical alteration amounted to a change of TOPS code and removal of the number prefix, either properly or just by painting them out. Full repaints were very rare, leading to wagons still carrying their engineers colours operating intermingled with those in Railfreight liveries.

ABOVE: With a lineage dating back to the Great Western Railway, the ZJV Mermaids were amazing if anachronistic survivors into privatisation, many passing to Transrail and then EWS. On September 10, 1997, Motherwell-allocated 37423 *Sir Murray Morrison* had strayed far from home as it passes Langley Mill with the 8E79 17.01 Mountsorrel-Doncaster conveying new ballast. The side-tippers would be out of traffic before the end of the decade. The Mermaid is currently found in the EFE Rail range in N gauge and exclusively from Footplate Models under its Flangeway brand, the OO gauge model being produced for it by Dapol. Phil Chilton

LEFT: The last vacuum-braked engineers' wagons to remain in traffic were the ZCV Clams. These were created in 1989/90 by fitting new box bodies onto underframes recovered from HTV hoppers, the robust nature and good condition of the fixed bodywork ensuring they lasted well. By February 26, 2002, the remaining wagons were nearing the end with 37670 captured shunting a rake at Chaddesden Sidings, Derby, following unloading of their spoil load. The Type 3 would later work the train back to Toton Yard. Curiously, from early 2000, EWS started a programme of reclassifying the Clams as mineral opens, these receiving the new TOPS code of MGV and having their DB number prefix painted out. Over 250 had been re-coded within 18 months although there was no great change in their deployment. Hornby offers the Clam in OO gauge, as does Peco in its Parkside kit range. Phil Chilton

RIGHT: The air braked ZBA Rudds were the natural successors to the ZBO/ZBV Grampus, finding nationwide usage following their conversion between 1989-91. These featured new drop-door bodies on reclaimed and overhauled underframes, the last examples serving until 2007 or so. A decade earlier, EWS-owned 31554 and 31185 pass Defford on September 15, 1996, having run-round at Gloucester while heading a spoil train away from a possession at Spetchley back to Bescot Yard. Once again, Hornby and Parkside are the modelling options In 4mm. Martin Loader

Modelling BR: Engineers Wagons of Privatisation

British Rail survivors

Vacuum brake decline

With the fate of the vacuum-braked engineers wagons sealed, Simon Bendall traces their demise under EWS with a selection of their final looks illustrated.

Despite British Rail's investment in replacement conversions, the short-wheelbase, two-axle, ballast and spoil opens still made up a considerable proportion of the vacuum-braked engineers' fleet during the mid-1990s. These were predominately wagons transferred to departmental use from the revenue fleet during the preceding decade, either without further modifications or with new bodies fitted on second-hand underframes.

Falling into the first of these categories were the ZKV Barbels, the former 27-ton tipplers having found considerable use under Mainline Freight, with EWS still having over 400 on its books come 1999. Frequently found working alongside them were the ZKV Zander, the former MTV sand wagons having been originally created in the mid-1970s by adding near indestructible box bodies to former private owner tank underframes. These numbered some 120 examples in 1999 but both fleets were all but gone within two years.

The ZCV TOPS code still covered a variety of different wagon types with the fate of the long-lived Clams already detailed on the previous page. None of the other designs lasted so long with Mainline Freight again being the main recipient of the Dace and Crab, which was unsurprising as they were historically Southern based. The Dace, as repurposed Shochoods, were some 35 years old when EWS took over and were all dispensed with almost immediately. In contrast, the much smaller fleet of Crabs had better bodywork as they dated from the early 1980s so eked out a living in the Midlands and finally Scotland to the end of the 1990s.

Also coming under ZCV were the Plaice, the rebodied plate wagons being of a similar vintage to the Crabs. Some 150 were still on EWS' books in 1999 working in the northwest, Midlands, and Scotland but their decline was similarly rapid thereafter. Finally, there were the Tope, the cut-down former 21-ton hoppers still numbering almost 700 examples in the same period, but they too were soon filling up scrapyards across the country.

Purpose-built decline

Of the ballast and spoil opens built specifically for the role by BR, only the Grampus made it to privatisation, particularly with Transrail and Loadhaul. Over 500 were still in EWS ownership at the end of the 1990s but a large quantity of these were in store awaiting disposal, which included a handful of unfitted examples. All of those still in traffic were vacuum braked but the type was extinct in service by 2001.

Transrail and then EWS briefly considered a life extension programme for the YCV Turbots as while the bodies were beaten and buckled, the former Bogie Bolster E underframes still had some life in them. DB978246 was given new fixed sides by Transrail in 1995, taking the codename of Heron, with two more known examples, DB978279 and DB978372, following under EWS. However, the wagons retained vacuum brakes so were at a disadvantage compared to creating more Sea Urchins, the latter route being preferred in the end. The trio were condemned alongside the Turbots, all being gone by early 2002.

Of the ballast hopper designs, the remaining ZEV Catfish were all withdrawn by 1999 as were the ZJV Mermaid side-tippers. In contrast, the ZFV Dogfish lasted two more years but some were deemed to be of further use, leading to 50 examples receiving air brakes at Wabtec, Doncaster, in late 2000 and early 2001. Recoded HPA, the hoppers retained their existing liveries, including Loadhaul black/orange, and were mainly found in the north of England, remaining in traffic until 2006 or so.

Alongside the purpose-built engineers fleet, various vacuum-braked former revenue earning wagons taken into departmental stock under BR also survived into privatisation as did some of the special wagons, such as Lowmacs and Flatrols. These all declined just as quickly, the latter especially as road/rail machinery was introduced. Ex revenue types that saw a few years' use included bogie bolsters of various types and open wagons, like 12-ton pipes and 22-ton tubes.

ABOVE: **Very few vacuum-braked engineers wagons received notable alterations after privatisation as they were clearly on borrowed time. An exception was YCV DB978246, which gained new fixed bodysides in 1995 as a prototype Heron. Originally finished in Transrail grey, it later gained EWS maroon and is seen in store at Taunton Fairwater Yard in June 1998. It had recently seen use on the rock armour workings to Minehead, conveying large boulders from Merehead and Whatley quarries for sea defence installation.** Hywel Thomas

British Rail survivors

ABOVE: The all-white Transrail 'T' logo was a common branding on engineers stock as displayed by ZBV Grampus DB991481 at Didcot in May 1998, its livery otherwise being rust. This is available in N and OO from Dapol with Parkside offering a kit in OO and O. Simon Bendall

ABOVE: Even more common was the Mainline lettering on a blue background as carried in the top left corner on ZCV Clam DB973135 at Guide Bridge on April 25, 1999. This was carrying old concrete sleepers. Hornby and Parkside both offer 4mm scale models. David Ratcliffe

ABOVE: With a livery predominately of rust, ZCV Plaice DB987233 was stabled at Crewe Gresty Lane on September 13, 1997. This sports white EWS branding on a black background, a common adornment that varied in size and style. No model exists in any scale. David Ratcliffe

ABOVE: Again carrying recovered concrete sleepers, ZKV Zander DB390067 was also at Guide Bridge on April 25, 1999, having seen its Mainline logo painted out. Revolution Trains released a N gauge model last year but there is no current version in OO gauge. David Ratcliffe

ABOVE: With a Transrail logo in place, ZCV Tope DB970630 was at Cockshute Sidings, Stoke, on March 23, 1998. As was commonplace on engineers stock, the lettering was becoming increasingly illegible due to rust and dirt. Hornby produces a model in 4mm. David Ratcliffe

ABOVE: The full colour Transrail logo adorning ZFV Dogfish DB983194 was far more unusual when recorded at Barry wagon repair depot on May 10, 1998. A warning notice to wear a respirator due to ballast dust also features by the operating platform at the far end. David Ratcliffe

RIGHT: Under Loadhaul ownership, a number of vacuum-braked ZFV Dogfish were overhauled, this including bodywork repairs and a repaint in the company's black and orange colours with white capping. Due to their good condition, many were subsequently selected by EWS to receive air brakes in 2000/01, the new equipment taking the place of the vacuum cylinder at one end of the underframe. On August 9, 2004, 993502 stands in Tyne Yard, having lost its DB prefix and gained the new TOPS code of HPA. Models of vacuum-braked Dogfish are available in 2mm from Dapol and Heljan in both 4mm and 7mm. Lee Davies

Modelling BR: Engineers Wagons of Privatisation 11

British Rail survivors

ABOVE: The two liveries carried by the ZKV Barbels at the end of their lives are typified by this duo with rust and scratches in evidence along with barely legible lettering.

A barrelful of Barbels

The former 27-ton tipplers were common on the erstwhile Western Region in the early years of privatisation so are perfect for James Makin's recreation of Didcot Parkway as he sets to work on a bevy of OO gauge Parkside kits.

The late 1990s were a period of great change for the engineering wagons tasked with conveying spoil, ballast, and sand to and from possessions as elderly vacuum-braked designs were replaced with large numbers of converted box-body air-braked wagons under new owners EWS. Casualties of the changes included the venerable ZKV Barbel wagons, which could be found on engineering trains across the Western Region until 1999, and the sight of the former iron ore tippler wagons contrasted sharply with the freshly applied privatised liveries of the new railway.

One of the last strongholds of the Barbels was Didcot Yard in Oxfordshire, where rakes would regularly be stabled between engineering possessions. Modelling this location therefore offered a compelling reason to tackle these anachronistic wagons in OO gauge.

While similar to the ready-to-run models offered by Bachmann and Hornby, these portray earlier builds with dimensional differences and, crucially, unfitted underframes without the necessary vacuum brake equipment. The only exact match for the MSV/ZKV Barbel in 4mm scale is through building the former Parkside Dundas kit, now marketed as part of the Peco range.

Construction tips

The kit itself fits together very easily using polystyrene cement and makes for a pleasing build as all of the parts are moulded with minimal flash. Each wagon was assembled over a piece of plate glass, which helps ensure they go together straight and level at all stages. Following the Peco instructions, the chassis was built up first, adding in the brass bearings to the sideframes and selecting the desired pattern of axlebox to represent your chosen examples. Many had the later BR hooded axlebox design, mouldings of which were obtained from Chivers Finelines and fixed in place.

ABOVE: Two of the Parkside kits under construction with the moulded buffer shanks having been removed from the ends.

The original buffers supplied with the kit were replaced by the finely moulded sprung examples produced as spares by Accurascale, which offers both the 13 inch BR Oleo design and the heavy-duty self-contained variety. One of the main areas where the kit can be improved is with the provision of additional brake detail. Strips

ABOVE: Like most vacuum-braked wagons, buffer and axlebox types varied considerably and it is here that after-market parts can be used to enhance what is supplied with the kit, such as these Chivers roller bearing boxes.

of 0.3mm brass wire were cut to shape to replicate the rods connecting the brake shoes together and pieces of 'U' shaped brass formed the safety loops around each axle, in each case superglued into small holes drilled in the chassis.

Smiths instanter couplings were fitted to the entire rake of Barbels, these being superglued in place after assembly. Each wagon received some additional weight in the form of liquid lead, which was poured into the base of the wagon.

ABOVE: Fitting additional brake details further enhances the underframe, such as the safety loops.

Tackling the liveries

By the late 1990s, the ZKVs had separated into two main types of livery, distressed engineers grey/yellow and extremely distressed bauxite! A significant proportion of the remaining Barbel fleet had received the former livery by the early 1990s, but this had deteriorated throughout the decade due to hard use and unloading by mechanical grabs, with resultant damage to the paintwork leading to rust patches forming on the sides. Others, meanwhile, had not been painted for many years. Notably, some of these bauxite examples still retained the

British Rail survivors

ABOVE: **Plastic wagon kits typically benefit from additional weight, liquid or fluid lead being a common option. If the wagons will always be loaded, this can be added inside.**

ABOVE: **Weathering of the bauxite examples is underway with shades of grey and brown being applied to the bodywork.**

ABOVE: **For the grey/yellow examples, shades of brown are the way to go, these also forming the scratch marks.**

remnants of the 'Iron Ore Tippler' branding on the bodysides amongst the numerous rusty brown shades.

With an eventual aim to model a long rake of 40 wagons, a start was made on the first batch of 11 models. Having looked through photos, the average ratio of grey/yellow to bauxite Barbels was approximately 60/40 respectively, so a representative seven of the 11 would feature the grey/yellow with the remainder being subjected to some extremely weathered brown shades.

Tackling the grey/yellow examples first, these were painted in a faded version of the livery to represent the wagons towards the end of their lives. A light grey was sprayed across each body followed by a pale yellow stripe to give a muted appearance to each of the wagons in this batch. For the bauxite wagons, a coating of Humbrol No. 62 Matt Leather was painted all over the body to give a good base for the later weathering stages.

Having waited for the base paintwork to dry, the next stage was to apply a coat of Railmatch gloss varnish to the wagon bodies, ready for the decals to be added. Railtec has now kindly produced a dedicated pair of transfer sets for the ZKV Barbels; however, these were not available at the time of modelling this batch of wagons, hence the need for some creativity!

On the grey/yellow versions, the TOPS panels were digitally created and printed onto a light grey backing, matched to the colour of each wagon, and stuck onto the bodies. Other decals including data panels and electrification flashes were then added, following prototype pictures for guidance.

When it came to the bauxite versions, the data panels were painstakingly created by hand from numbering sheets from Fox and Railtec, and the 'Iron Ore Tippler' lettering from the decals supplied with the kit by Peco.

Going forward, the new decals from Railtec will make future batches much easier to complete as they include fully made-up TOPS panels and the correct types of data panels ready to apply. With decals applied, each wagon was given a coat of Railmatch matt varnish and left for a month for the surface to harden before weathering could begin.

Weathering & battering

By the late 1990s, the condition of the Barbel fleet was extremely poor with most wagons exhibiting large amounts of flaking paint, dents, scars and rust bubbling through the faded paintwork, so weathering these was a critical part of creating a believable privatisation era train.

For the bauxite-liveried wagons, by the end of their careers, the finish on the wagon body was a very dark grey, almost black appearance, so this was replicated by applying a series of increasingly dark brown and dark grey shades to the body. This was mottled on with a brush, sometimes over the top of the previous layer of wet paint to blend and build up the shades in certain areas, matching all the time to prototype pictures. Humbrol enamel paints were utilised throughout the process, including Nos. 62, 186, 113, 133, 251 and 32. Additionally, some use of Phoenix Precision Paints' No. P216 Virgin Trains dark grey came in handy for the very dark areas on the wagons - who would have thought it!

The design of the wagons also led to greater levels of weathering in certain areas, particularly where rainwater was drawn down the sides due to capillary action. The more sheltered parts of the body underneath the framing also weathered differently, so it is important to always work from photos of specific wagons.

For the grey/yellow-liveried wagons, the initial weathering process was simpler than the bauxite versions but the lighter colours showed up numerous scratches and damage which all needed to be modelled. Two layers

ABOVE: **The original 'Iron Ore Tippler' branding is barely visible beneath the dirt with the layers of weathering shades applied over the top of the transfer.**

Modelling BR: Engineers Wagons of Privatisation 13

British Rail survivors

ABOVE: The fine ballast produced by Woodland Scenics makes a useful wagon load with weathering further enhancing the look.

of paint-on/wipe-off washes were applied onto these wagons, a light brown, typically Humbrol No. 62, and a mid-brown, such as Humbrol Nos. 186 or 113.

The paint was mixed 60/40 with enamel thinners and applied all over the body, before being removed with kitchen towel, wiping vertically downwards to remove the bulk of the paint. This will leave paint in the recesses of the wagon to represent the dirt that does not get washed away by the rain. Several days were left between coats of the paint wash to allow the layers to harden before going over with the next shade. Building up several layers enhances the appearance of the weathered finish with a greater range of tones visible.

Next, the distinctive scratches, scrapes and body damage was replicated using a fine 5/0 paintbrush. When being unloaded by a mechanical grab, often the damage to the inside of the body would create a slight crease, blistering the paint on the outside of the wagon body and allowing water ingress and rust patches to form.

The rust patches were emulated using multiple shades of brown, in this case the five shades of Humbrol employed earlier, namely Nos. 62, 186, 113, 133 and 251. The very lightest shade was applied to the scrape or rust patch first, then working up to the very darkest shade at the epicentre of the rust patch. It can be a slow process applying tiny amounts of paint over the top of each other but once the multiple shades are applied, the resulting effect is very pleasing to the eye.

Finishing touches

The inside of each wagon was weathered using a similar palette of colours, building up the shades to match photos and then dry-brushing some light grey shades over the top to replicate the dust left behind from a spoil or ballast load.

Moving down to the chassis, for each wagon this was painted in a combination of dark grey, black and dark brown, these being mottled onto the underframe and blended together while wet until satisfied with the overall appearance. Certain areas such as the axleboxes and moving parts are covered in oil, so these were treated to some Humbrol Metalcote gunmetal to bring out an oily sheen. Axlebox identification colours were added as required and the final wagon in the rake was fitted with a cosmetic tail-lamp as well as a vacuum brake pipe.

Finally, loads were added using Woodland Scenics fine ballast, which was glued in place with PVA over some Peco plastic load-formers to give a peaked effect to the loads. The ballast was then given a weathering with thinned down paint dropped into the dried ballast load, which gives the appearance of dirty and used ballast spoil. Each wagon then received a final coat of Railmatch matt varnish to seal in the weathering and protect them against the rigours of exhibition life.

ABOVE: Two more bauxite examples illustrate the wide variety found in lettering styles with one having boxed lettering and the other being unboxed.

ABOVE: Despite the decline of vacuum-braked stock, early 1999 saw EWS run a series of driver refresher runs from Old Oak Common to remind crews how to handle such wagons. These ran in a loop via the Berks & Hants, Melksham and Didcot with Class 31 power. On March 17, 1999, DB388447 in grey/yellow with Mainline branding and bauxite DB388334 roll through Didcot on the way back to London. *Simon Bendall*

British Rail survivors

Air brake developments

Privatisation brought new looks for the ex BR air-braked engineers fleet with overhauls, repaints and re-codings. Simon Bendall **looks at the colourful results.**

In contrast with the vacuum-braked fleet, the air-braked engineers wagons were largely retained 'as is' by the three regional freight companies and then EWS in its earliest years, at least until higher capacity replacements began to arrive.

By the mid-1990s, the Sealions and Seacows were the principal ballast hoppers at work on the network and the companies continued with the modernisation programme implemented by BR earlier in the decade. One aspect of this was to remove the vacuum-brake equipment fitted to many of the riveted-body YGH Sealions as this was now all but redundant.

This concerned wagons in the DB982440-927 series and the work either saw the retention of a through vacuum pipe, bringing recoding as YGB, or as became favoured later in the decade, the complete removal of the vacuum system including a through pipe, resulting in the new TOPS code of YGA. No matter which modification was carried out, the altered wagons also took the revised name of Seacow.

The welded-bodied YGB Seacows dating from 1981/82, DB980000-250, were already air-braked only but had been built with a through vacuum pipe for compatibility with older stock, so this also tended to be removed during overhaul, the hoppers becoming YGA. Overhauled wagons of both body types were variously repainted in Mainline, Loadhaul and Transrail colours before EWS maroon took over.

The other main modification was to fit electric lighting beneath the safety canopy over the operating platforms, this requiring the addition of conduit runs, inter-wagon jumper cables and electrical boxes. To provide power, one wagon per set was fitted with a compact diesel generator at one end, these being named Stingray. Some attempt was made to keep the modified wagons in fixed sets, such as by Mainline Freight, but this was only partially successful. In some cases, the safety canopies were also given side extensions to improve protection, but this was not universal.

Shark refurbishment

Although the number of ZUV Shark ballast ploughs in traffic had declined, a sizeable number were still required to work with the Seacows, Stingrays, Whales, and remaining Dogfish. A number of these also saw refurbishment during the 1990s to overcome the twin issues of rotten bodywork and vacuum brakes. This included replacing the vacuum brakes with air, either with or without a through vacuum pipe, resulting in the revised codes of ZUB and ZUA, respectively.

Some Sharks were additionally either fully or partially reskinned using plywood instead of planks while, as they no longer served as conventional brake vans, the stove and chimney were often removed. Mainline and Loadhaul both applied their colours to a small number of overhauled vehicles as did EWS, this coming in several styles depending on which workshop was responsible.

One Shark, DB993806, saw its bodywork completely removed in 1999 in favour of receiving metal handrails all round and a mesh roof but the conversion was not repeated. During 2001/02, around 25 Sharks that had retained vacuum brakes had the equipment removed, rendering them unfitted with a through air pipe. The affected vans were recoded RUQ and lost the DB prefix from their numbers.

Other types

The YHA Whales were not treated to the lighting upgrades given to their smaller cousins so were all but gone by 2005 as the autoballasters usurped them. The YBA Sturgeon and YPA Tench similarly declined rapidly in the mid-2000s as they were replaced, their elderly bogie design counting against them along with life-expired bodywork. In contrast, the Salmons continued to serve in large numbers, EWS going so far as to invest in fitting new ASF cast bogies to overcome the type's main limitation from 1999, the widespread programme bringing recoding initially as YSA and YWA.

Other types, such as the ZBA Rudd and ZCA Seahorse, continued into the mid-2000s as did the ZFA Gunnell and ZKA Limpet, EWS conducting some recoding of the latter two types as HGA and MKA respectively as they also found use on commercial freight duties such as sand and coal. Lastly, the YLA Mullet remained in use until late 2022 while the remaining YQA Parr still serve today.

ABOVE: Fresh from overhaul, ballast hopper T982766 is now a YGB Seacow following the removal of its vacuum brakes and recoding from a YGH Sealion. It has also seen its DB number prefix removed in favour of a T, this indicating Transrail ownership, although when seen at Crianlarich on May 25, 1996, behind 37232, it was now an EWS asset. The wagon has additionally received the side extensions to its safety canopies but not lighting, while the grey with red stripe was Transrail's favoured livery for its Seacows. Kernow Model Rail Centre has released this livery as a limited edition in OO gauge. Simon Bendall Collection

Modelling BR: Engineers Wagons of Privatisation **15**

British Rail survivors

ABOVE: Generator-fitted Stingray DB982477 is seen at Didcot in May 2000, this carrying Mainline Freight blue while the '3' on the side indicated it was originally part of light-fitted set 3. The jumper cable connections and associated electrical conduit can be seen on the end.

ABOVE: Finished in Mainline blue, Shark DB993842 had seen both its sides and verandas re-skinned with plywood, leaving just the doors retaining planking. It has also been converted to air brakes but without a through vacuum pipe. Seen at Didcot in May 1999.

ABOVE: Also found at Didcot in June 2000, DC390648 was typical of the ZFA Gunnells, these largely retaining grey/yellow apart from the handful of Mainline blue repaints. The former Mainline branding has been painted out towards the right hand end of the wagon.

ABOVE: The ZCA Seahorse were amongst the first ballast wagons to be converted from air-braked opens, in this case OCAs. With the later conversion of the Sea Urchins, they were operationally regarded as the same with DC112140 pictured between two such wagons at Didcot.

ABOVE: Loadhaul opted to create more ZCA Sea Hare in preference to Sea Urchins, sealing the doors shut on SPA and ZAA Pike by adding metal strips across the top. In the company's colours, DC460179 arrives at Didcot on August 4, 2000, with its sides already badly rusted.

ABOVE: The former Satlink fleet largely passed to the regional freight companies and then EWS with many returned to their previous revenue codes. Now back as an OCA, 112192 displays some interesting fading effects to its paintwork at Didcot in June 2000. Simon Bendall

ABOVE: DB984788 was one of the Grampus converted to a ZBA Rudd by BR on the cheap by fitting air brakes and new solid ends. Possibly unique in receiving EWS colours, it passes Portway on May 16, 2002. The 4mm Parkside kit will produce this variant. Gareth Bayer

ABOVE: Definitely a one-off was the Loadhaul-liveried ZBA Rudd, DB972644 being recorded at Peterborough on April 7, 2004, when owned by EWS. Something of a 'celebrity' in the wagon world, Hornby has produced the wagon RTR in OO gauge. Gareth Bayer

British Rail survivors

ABOVE: Hornby is the only source of the welded-body Seacow hoppers in 4mm scale, while the older riveted body Sealion design is offered by both Bachmann and Hornby, the latter being the elderly Lima model. The main line career of the last set of Seacows, which included both body types, came to an end in 2017 with their withdrawal by DB Cargo. By this date, they were beaten, battered, rusty and filthy!

A sting in the tale

To power the light fitted Seacows, several of the hoppers received compact diesel generator sets, these being designated Stingrays. Timara Easter describes how to detail the Hornby model and give it a Transrail makeover.

I seem to have a lot of one-off wagons in my collection, this Stingray being no exception. I have yet to find another example of one of the 1980s-build of welded body Seacows painted in the uninspiring Transrail grey livery, especially converted into a generator-fitted example such as this, the company preferring to enliven things with a red stripe.

The modifications to the Hornby model were relatively straightforward, beginning by creating the cage for the generator from an early Shawplan Class 56 bodyside grille. This was suitably cut, formed, and soldered using photos as a reference before placing it in the required space, which is at the opposite end to the brake gear. The outside inspection panel was made from a piece of 20 thou plasticard, the dimensions again estimated from photos.

The electrical conduits on the ends were made from 0.4mm brass wire formed into shape and threaded through the junction boxes, which were created using 1mm/40 thou plastic strip. These were all secured in place with superglue. The light under each protective canopy mesh was made from 1.5mm/60 thou plasticard, being drilled at one end to accept 0.4mm wire as per the end conduits.

One last little job at the generator end of the model was to carefully reposition the incorrectly placed lamp bracket as Hornby put it on the wrong side of the coupling hook. This applies to the Seacows as well and then allows the air brake pipe to go in the correct position.

Painting
Once all the work was done, the buffers were masked and the body primed in Halfords grey followed by painting in Humbrol No. 126 grey, which is close enough to the shade used by Transrail. The solebars were next painted black and then the relevant areas picked out in white and orange. Transfers were a mix of Fox (logos), Modelmaster (overhead warning flashes) and Appleby (numbering).

Replacement couplings came from the Smiths range, which were fitted after painting, and air pipes from my spares box. Since I model in EM gauge, the wheels were changed for those from Steam Era Models, as used for Black Beetle motor bogies, with all but the treads blackened before fitting into the bogies.

Generally, ballast hoppers got very grubby quite quickly, although this one is portrayed not long after its repaint around 1995. I started with a wash of Humbrol Nos. 62 and 27004, gently streaking in a downwards motion and removing almost all of it. The ballast chutes were given a wash of burnt sienna gouache from Winsor & Newton, which I later streaked while drying. A light dusting of MIG 'Europe Dust' helped tone the chute colour down a little while also simulating the effect of ballast dust.

A slightly lighter mix of the same two Humbrol colours was then built up on the bogies to give the effect of track and brake dirt, while a final misting across the whole model with an airbrush helped blend it all together.

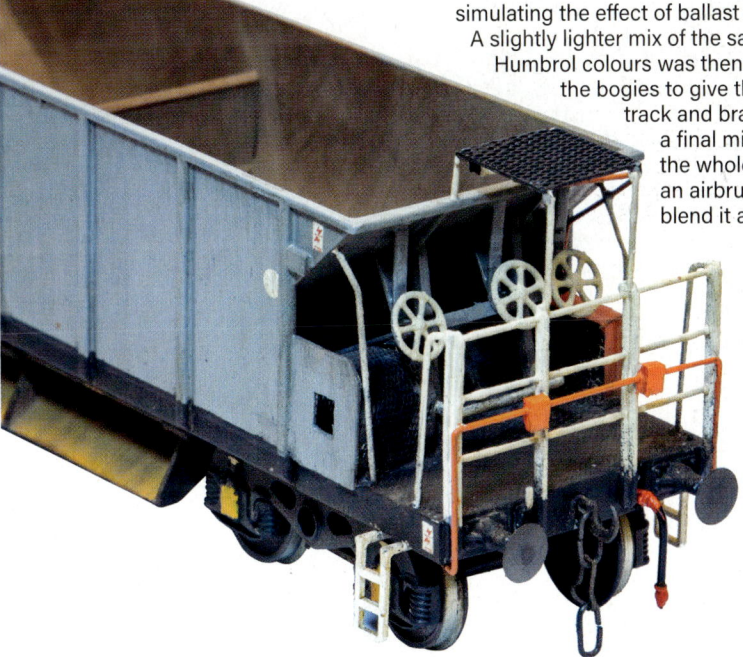

ABOVE: The generator set on a Stingray was tucked in under the hopper at one end and covered by mesh to protect it from rogue lumps of ballast. The metal plate on the side gave access to the controls while the orange switchbox on the far side and the end electrical conduit were common to the light-fitted wagons. The conduit also ran up to the light beneath the canopy, all recreated here.

British Rail survivors

ABOVE: 110301 displays a mix of paint and unpainted wood, the latter recreating the dark grey look of the weathered planks.

Technicolour OBAs

With the ZDA Bass returned to revenue stock as OBAs by EWS, the fleet of wooden-bodied open wagons sported an array of liveries by the late 1990s. However, with maroon repaints soon curtailed, they descended into patchwork quilts of colours as repairs were carried out. James Makin describes how to model a selection using the OO gauge Bachmann model.

First introduced in 1974 as part of BR's new air-braked wagon fleet, the wooden-bodied OBA open wagons were starting to show their two decades of service by the time privatisation arrived. The wagons were useful for a wide variety of engineering jobs, such as carrying sleepers, lightweight plant and equipment, aggregates bags and similar, while they were equally good for removing all manner of detritus from worksites.

However, the wooden doors were a vulnerability and subject to frequent damage, resulting in numerous patch repairs and plank replacements over the years. These new planks were often painted in whatever colour came to hand, if they were painted at all, so that by the mid-1990s, an OBA could sport several colours on the sides. This only got worse under EWS as budgets were tightened and full repaints ceased, the wagons descending into mobile advertisements for Dulux!

In 4mm scale, Cambrian has long offered a plastic kit, which was supplemented by Bachmann's RTR model in 2006, and it is the latter that forms the basis of the models featured here. Bachmann's model is readily available and used examples can be picked up for very reasonable sums.

Getting started

As the Bachmann OBA is very well moulded and requires minimal additional work, this leaves plenty of time available for weathering and personalising the wagons to replicate the many images that can be found across Flickr, SmugMug and Google Images. Having selected a number of examples to recreate in miniature, the next step was to apply the various liveries.

The Bachmann printing can be scraped away with a curve-bladed scalpel and the planks repainted where required using paints of the modeller's choice. In this case, Humbrol enamels were mixed by eye to

ABOVE: The initial painting of the planks, ends, and solebars is underway, this providing the basis on which to add the weathering effects.

the faded shades required for each model. Where there were planks in different colours, the base colour was painted on using a fine brush, getting as close to the final colour as possible, and then any fine tuning made later on during the weathering stages. As part of the project, an ex-Satlink example was chosen, which proved to be especially interesting when replicating the various faded shades of red and yellow as the livery had deteriorated significantly since application.

Once the base paint finish was completed, each model received a coat of Railmatch gloss varnish before the transfers were applied. The TOPS panels were created on a computer, being sketched out in CorelDraw, and printed on photo paper, and then supplemented by data panels and electrification flashes from Fox Transfers. Finally, a coat of Railmatch matt varnish was sprayed all over the body to seal in the decals

Rust and washes

A significant part of modelling an OBA is recreating the battered and unloved appearance of the prototypes, so it was great fun to start work on these. The first step was to apply a set of washes to highlight the recesses between the wooden planks and also to represent the damaged and rusty condition of the metal ends.

Neat layers of Humbrol enamel paint were applied, beginning with Nos. 62, 186 and 113. This was painted on and wiped vertically downwards with a kitchen towel and cotton buds, allowing for a couple of days drying time between different paint shades. This helps to bring out the plank detail as desired and can also create rust streaking from exposed metal items such as the door bangers and restraint chains as part of the process.

A series of light brown paint washes was then applied to the metal ends of the OBAs and once dry, they were then dry brushed with light and medium shades of brown to highlight damage to the exposed edges of

ABOVE: Graffiti outnumbers the amount of paint left on the side of 110073, this being painted on freehand using a variety of colours.

British Rail survivors

ABOVE: Once a ZDA Bass, 110199 was one of the wagons re-coded back to an OBA by EWS, this also having its allocated pool number added to the solebar.

ABOVE: Weathering of the planks is in progress with the grey being dry brushed on horizontally to create the grain detail.

the raised ribs. Later, individual marks and rust patches were added using fine 5/0 paintbrushes. The rust patches were created using shades of brown, namely Humbrol Nos. 62, 186, 113, 133 and 251, dabbing on the lightest shade with a dry brush and working up to the darkest shade at the epicentre of the rust outbreak.

Plank weathering
The process for recreating weathered wood, especially bare unpainted planks, is very different to that for other materials. Observation is key so it is useful to look at how wood weathers in real life; a garden fence can be great inspiration close up and useful for the modeller to see just how many shades are involved, these ranging from light grey to almost silver.

Following prototype photos, the planking was first painted in a dark brown shade, and while still tacky, a dry brush of light grey was dragged along the plank working in the direction of the wood grain, which in this case is horizontally along the wagon. More shades of grey were added using the same dry-brushing technique, starting with a medium grey and working lighter to an almost off-white shade, building up the layers one at a time until satisfied. Occasionally, other shades of brown were gently added on top in select places to create some tonal variation, but the overall effect is a silver-grey appearance.

On the painted planks, there is often traces of mould and rot getting under the painted finish and causing it to flake away.

This necessitated the use of the fine 5/0 paintbrushes to recreate, gently dabbing on colour where needed with each extra tone building up on the weathered finish for a more realistic result. With a wagon type as varied as the OBAs, there are no hard and fast rules as each wagon is entirely unique, so the most important part to take away is to religiously examine the photos of a chosen prototype and recreate the exact range of colours, damage and patches that can be seen on a specific date.

Interiors & underframes
The inside of each wagon was painted in a range of light browns and then weathered further with dark greys, these being painted on and wiped away in a vertical motion. Where there are replacement planks on the outside, these should be painted on the inside as well using the same light grey weathering described above.

On the underframe, this was painted in a mottled range of browns and dark greys, as well as touching in the axlebox covers with an identification colour where required and adding silver chrome on the buffer shanks.

The wheelsets were also given attention with Stenson Models brake discs applied to each wheel face, these being glued in place with PVA and then subjected to a paint-on/wipe-off finish with dark grey paint to highlight the bolt detail on each disc. Each wheel and axle assembly was then painted in a suitable dark grey/brown shade with the wheel treads then cleaned and left to dry. Each wagon was lastly given an overall coat of Railmatch matt varnish to finish, with the models then good to enter service.

ABOVE: The next stage is to add a recreation of the flaking paint to the plank edges, this requiring close attention to be paid to photos for reference.

ABOVE: The Satlink livery suffered particularly badly from the effects of weathering with the red fading to salmon pink. 110058 displays evidence of this in addition to fresher red from plank repairs.

Modelling BR: Engineers Wagons of Privatisation **19**

British Rail survivors

Mesh-sided OAA/OBA

Under EWS ownership, a number of former BR open wagons were rebuilt with mesh sides for Mendip Rail block traffic and then infrastructure services. Gareth Bayer gives a rundown of their history.

Built between 1971 and 1979, the OAA and OBA open wagons have seen more than a few modifications since their introduction. One of the most radical was first unveiled in 1998 with EWS replacing the wooden doors on a number of OAAs before doing the same on numerous OBAs. This overcame the traditional weak point of the two designs and helped ensure their longevity. As a result, the final OAA in traffic, 100048, was only withdrawn at the beginning of 2023 after 50 years in service, while a dwindling number of OBAs are still in use.

The mesh side modification was first developed after Mendip Rail introduced a new concrete block service for Forticrete between Merehead Quarry and Acton, this initially employing wooden-sided OAA and OBA wagons. As the sides were very vulnerable to damage from the heavy blocks, a batch of OAAs were given three drop-side mesh doors of the same size as the wooden ones they replaced. Initially, 19 wagons were converted with a further group of 12 following soon after.

The 31 vehicles, 100000/7/9/10/2-5/20-2/7/37/46/52/4/6/65/9-72/6/8/9/81/4/91/5/7/9,

ABOVE: **The final vehicle in the 7A09 Merehead-Acton 'Jumbo' train at Reading on March 7, 2002, was loaded Mendip Pool OAA 100081. The first application of the replacement mesh sides, the OAAs in this pool were used on concrete block traffic. The adjoining wagon is an un-rebuilt OBA in EWS livery, still with its extended Plasmor ends.** Gareth Bayer

were coded OAA-F, while 100027 was of note as it retained its extended height ends from its days carrying Redland roof tiles. All gained maroon number panels, Mendip Pool placards and EWS logo plates on the mesh sides. The new mesh was also painted maroon, while all lettering was in EWS gold with the exception of the last seven conversions, 100000/10/3/22/84/91/9, which were given white panels with black lettering. The wagons otherwise remained in their former paint schemes.

Initially running as a direct service, by 1999 the block carriers were being tagged onto the rear of Mendip Rail's 'Jumbo' services. The mesh sided OAAs were also used on block traffic between Camas' Croft Quarry and Bow terminal in East London and were later recorded working between Peak Forest and Ely.

Super Bass

The OAA and OBA fleets were no strangers to infrastructure use. BR had transferred large numbers of both types to the Civil Engineer and other departmental divisions in the 1980s and they were typically given

ABOVE: **OAA 100080 was one of the 17 examples converted at Thornaby under the Super Bass programme in 2007. Featuring a different style of number panel, they were intended for infrastructure traffic from the outset. Captured at Salop Goods Junction, Crewe, on July 21, 2012, the wooden floor is littered with bits of packing material from a previous sleeper load.** Mark Franklin

20 www.keymodelworld.com

British Rail survivors

ABOVE: **Like a number of other wagon conversion programmes over the years, only minimal painting was conducted on the mesh sided OAA and OBA wagons. Captured at Didcot on August 31, 2012, OBA 110026 clearly betrays its previous engineers' grey and yellow livery. The modified OBAs retained four drop doors per side, compared to the three of the OAAs.** Mark Franklin

ABOVE: **OBA 110109 displays its modified door at the right hand end at Hinksey Yard on March 8, 2015. As well as the steps partly replacing the mesh, there are two additional handrails to assist staff in climbing onboard the wagon. Stacks of new concrete or steel sleepers were a typical load for the wagons as were recovered timber sleepers loaded less neatly.** Rich Martin

the new TOPS code of ZDA with the codename of Squid (ex OAA) or Bass (ex OBA). The majority of these became part of the EWS fleet at privatisation and they were quickly returned to their original TOPS codes, although they were still primarily employed for carrying infrastructure materials.

In mid-2007, 17 OAAs (100002/4/5/24/30/1/3/42/5/8/50/61/8/80/2/96/8) were given mesh doors in two batches at Thornaby carriage and wagon shops. The new sides were identical to those fitted to the Mendip Rail vehicles and these were again the only parts that received a repaint. The lettering was restricted to just a maroon TOPS number panel with the pertinent information being stencilled somewhat crudely in white, although some vehicles also received duplicate information on the solebars. These received the same OAA-F TOPS code as the Mendip examples and were allocated to EWS Network, later DB, pool 6812 for OAA/OBA Super Bass.

Later in 2007, the first OBA opens were also rebuilt with mesh sides, with both Warrington Arpley and Wigan Springs Branch undertaking the conversions. Like the modified OAAs, the four replacement doors used the original door stanchions and were of similar size to the original wooden fittings. They even included bump stops welded to the mesh. The wagons were allocated the new code of OBA-M, and, in most cases, the numbers and data panels were neatly applied to the base of the former body in white on a black panel. They were transferred to the same pool as the OAAs.

Sixty four wagons were converted, namely 110004/23/6/9/37/45/60/4/71/6/86, 110100/9/13/23/42/6/7/54/6/70/3/4, 110201-3/10/2/9/26/9/32/3/83/91/8, 110313/5/25/30/3/70/2/83, 110412/26/41/51/8/72, 110545/88, 110618/28/69/97, 110706/33/49/50/5/8/73 and 110800. The modifications were completed by the end of 2008 with 110545 and 110618 being former Plasmor rebuilds with the extended ends.

Deployment

The mesh sided OAA and OBA opens were used interchangeably and could be found on exactly the same sort of trains they were used on before rebuilding, with steel and concrete sleepers a typical load. They were often intermingled with wooden-sided OAAs and OBAs, steel-sided OCAs, YQA Super Tench and other infrastructure wagon types.

Around 2010, a number of the Super Bass were further modified with the mesh on the right hand door of each side being cut back and three steps added in its place, these providing easy access to the wagon deck when the sides were lowered. Accompanying handrails were also fitted to the ends, one on the OAAs and two on the OBAs. Based on photographs, at least the following were converted: 100002/4/30/50/68, 110023/71, 110109/13/23/46/56, 110201/2/10/2/9/32/3/83/98, 110313/5/30/72/83, 110441/58, 110545, 110697 and 110733/49. Around the same time, the wagons received black paint on the door stanchions and sides of the doors.

Aluminium-sided OBA

Although not fitted with mesh sides, OBA 110018 was given new aluminium doors in 1998 as an experiment, these being finished in grey and to the same size as its original wooden ones. The modified wagon was first put to work on the concrete block flow for Mendip Rail, initially with unconverted OAAs and OBAs.

It was given EWS maroon painted sides in the early 2000s, possibly as a result of a graffiti attack. By the mid-2000s, it was stored at Old Oak Common and famously loaded with a spare Class 67 cab shell. By the end of the decade, with the run-down of the West London depot well underway, it was moved to Toton.

RIGHT: **The aluminium-doored OBA prototype 110018 spent a number of years stored at Old Oak Common, during which time it carried a spare Class 67 cab. By August 30, 2008, it was dumped at the rear of the Factory and disappearing into the undergrowth.** Simon Bendall

Modelling BR: Engineers Wagons of Privatisation **21**

British Rail survivors

ABOVE: A combination of styrene sheet and strip along with etched brass and mesh can turn the Bachmann OBA into a modern re-doored example.

Meshing with an OBA

Seeking to add some variety to an engineers' train, James Makin describes how to convert the OO gauge Bachmann wagon to feature mesh sides using simple scratchbuilding.

For an infrastructure train on Worthing MRC's Loftus Road layout, I decided to model one of the mesh-sided OBA wagons to provide a bit of variation within the train. I chose wagon 110173 as the subject, this being finished in a light grey colour scheme and featuring heavy rust staining.

On paper, the project seemed straightforward, simply requiring the removal of the sides from the existing Bachmann OBA body. However, once these were cut away, it became apparent that Bachmann's model is hiding a secret! Namely, the floor sits too high in the wagon. To get around this, the old floor was put to one side and a new one fabricated from styrene sheet, measuring 137mm by 31.5mm and cut from 1mm thick plastic.

The existing Bachmann ends were then carefully cut away with a razor saw and attached to the new floor. The assembly

ABOVE: The first job is to remove the planked sides of the Bachmann OBA by cutting them away from the ends and underframe.

ABOVE: With the sides cut away, the height issue with the floor is clear to see, it extends up to the level of the first bodyside plank.

was then mated with the chassis, taking care to ensure that the solvent dried without bubbling the new styrene flooring.

Adding the mesh

Moving on to the 'party piece' of the wagon, the mesh sides are etched brass grilles applied over a brass framework, the latter holding the wagon together. With the wagon ends glued to the floor, two pieces of 140mm 'L' shape brass section were cut and affixed between the two ends at 11mm from the wagon floor, forming the top guide rails. Grooves were cut into the plastic Bachmann ends to accommodate the 'L'-shape sections.

ABOVE: To remedy the floor issue, a new, thinner one needs to be fabricated from plastic sheet, to which the Bachmann ends are then glued.

Strips of 1.5mm square styrene strip were then added to the bottom of the sides, which work in conjunction with the 'L'-shape brass to make a frame for the mesh sides to sit in once complete. Three vertical pillars measuring 4mm x 11mm x 1mm were added to each of the sides, using prototype pictures to ensure accurate spacing. With the frames completed, the next task was to cut Shawplan etched brass chequered sheets into 32mm by 9mm pieces, these were then fixed in place on the framework using superglue to form the sides.

ABOVE: The first elements of the new side framework are in place, these being the upper brass 'L' section and the lower plasticard strips.

The real mesh has a fine framework to give additional support. This could be added by using very fine styrene strip, but I opted for a simpler method. Microscale Krystal Klear was used to infill sections of the brass mesh to create the appearance that there was a framework behind the etched brass. Although clear when dried, once painted this would give the desired effect.

Sections of styrene were then attached on the outside of the door pillars along with representations of the chains securing each door. Finally, additional pieces of 8.5mm styrene were added to replicate the door bangers on the underframe. With the body detailing completed, it was time to move on to the finishing.

British Rail survivors

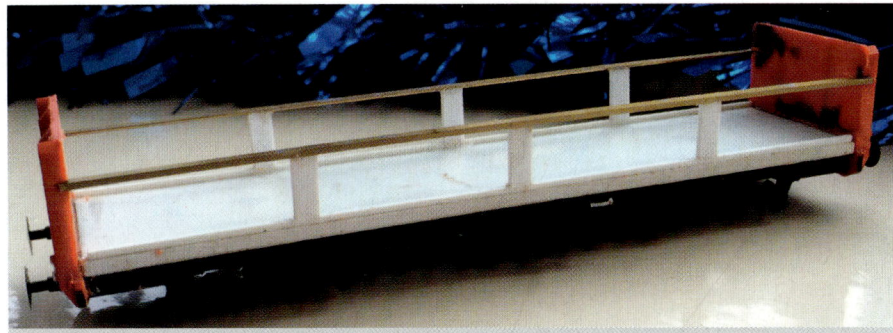

ABOVE: The next job on the sides is to add the door pillars, again from plastic. The spacing of these should be judged using photographs.

ABOVE: The first section of door mesh glued in place; this being made using cut down etched grilles produced by Shawplan.

Livery and weathering

The OBA body was first painted in Phoenix Precision's P957 Cement Rendering light grey across all surfaces and then left to dry. The weathering was built up in layers using the common 'apply and wipe off' technique. Almost neat paint was applied to the model and removed with varying degrees of vigour using either kitchen towel or cotton buds where appropriate.

Starting with the lightest colours first, a coat of Humbrol No. 62 Matt Leather was applied and wiped down. Leaving behind a streaky appearance, coats of No. 186 Matt Brown and No. 32 Dark Grey followed this. From observing the prototype, rusty stains are typically lighter at the edges and darker at the centre, so by applying the lightest colours first you can then concentrate the darker shades at the source of the rust patch. Similar colours were also applied by dry brushing to highlight key areas prone to rust along with the panelling on the floor.

The underframe was weathered using a mixture of various browns, greys, white and black, these being 'dolloped' into a foil dish and then mottled onto the wagon with a larger paintbrush. By mottling, you can blend the shades together but bias the tone of the paint depending on where you are working, for example brake dust deposits around the wheels.

It was unusual to find a standard TOPS panel on a modern OBA with hastily applied stencils or hand-painted elements being more common. 110173 was no different, having a smaller identification panel with hand-painted numbers. Suitable handwritten data panels were created in CorelDraw before being applied to the model and then subjected to further weathering.

Finishing touches including adding etched brake discs from Stenson Models and electrification flashes from Fox Transfers. Once completed, the entire wagon was then coated in Humbrol matt varnish to seal in the weathering and transfers, ready for its new life on Loftus Road.

ABOVE: A close-up of the doors shows how the Krystal Klear applied to the mesh effectively creates the vertical and horizontal strengthening ribs once the paint is applied.

ABOVE: Finishing touches on the sides include adding strengthening ribs to the door pillars and new door bangers on the underframe.

ABOVE: The completed mesh-sided OBA ready for painting. Invariably, the modified wagons retained their existing livery on the ends with the new doors finished in EWS maroon but there were exceptions.

ABOVE: The aluminium doored prototype 110018 can also be modelled from the Bachmann OBA, initially by judicious filling of the plank detail and then sanding down to achieve a smooth finish. The wagon was then painted using silver-white for the doors and EWS maroon for the remainder with the transfers again homemade.

Modelling BR: Engineers Wagons of Privatisation 23

British Rail survivors

ABOVE: A Loadhaul-liveried Limpet shows the look of the wagons under EWS ownership with the side cut-outs in place but now coded as a MKA and without a prefix to the number.

Livening up Limpets

Rebuilding and reusing were common themes among engineers' wagons, the ZKA/MKA Limpets that were converted by both BR and the regional freight companies being a prime example of this. James Makin tackles a selection of models using the 4mm scale Bachmann wagon.

During the mid-1980s, batches of surplus TTA tankers were rebuilt as aggregates wagons, these seeing their barrels removed and the underframes receive new box bodies. Coded POA and PNA, they were employed by the likes of ARC and Foster Yeoman and also saw some deployment on coal traffic.

With the arrival of high capacity replacements, many of the POAs and PNAs were sold to BR in the early 1990s and redeployed as spoil wagons, allowing numerous older designs to be withdrawn. In an effort to prevent overloading with water-logged spoil, two distinctive slots were cut into each side to restrict the amount that could be loaded. Reclassified as ZKA Limpets in the DC390150-331 number range, the conversions were done on a tight budget and while early examples received a full coat of grey and yellow on the sides, many later wagons received only a partial repaint, leaving their previous plain grey, Yeoman grey or ARC mustard liveries discernible beneath the grime and rust.

At privatisation, the fleet was split between the three regional freight companies with Loadhaul and Transrail turning out examples in their respective black/orange and plain grey liveries. Mainline Freight was more reluctant to splash the paint for once but at least one example did receive blue with yellow capping.

Not all of the POAs and PNAs available had become Limpets by the time BR was broken up, Loadhaul instead taking these on for use on coal traffic. These were reclassified as MKAs and renumbered 393000-035, some received Loadhaul repaints but not all. The MKAs differed from the ZKA Limpets as they did not have the overloading slots cut in the sides as with coal being less dense that spoil, the wagons could be loaded to capacity.

Under EWS ownership, the distinction between the two fleets became blurred and complicated with some ZKA Limpets initially having their bodyside slots temporarily plated over to join the MKAs on commercial traffic. However, during the early 2000s, all of the ZKA Limpets remaining in service in the 390150-331 series were reclassified as MKAs and lost their DC number prefixes as part of EWS' drive to reduce the number of departmental TOPS codes. At the same time, the original MKAs, 393000-035, had the overloading slots cut into their sides with the resulting combined fleet all deployed on spoil traffic thereafter. Further changes would later take place, but these are detailed in the MTA section on pages 48-49.

Modelling Limpets

With that hopefully cleared up, a natural starting point for the Limpets is the Bachmann model. Over the years, the manufacturer has produced a number of versions and liveries, including the original POA/PNA and MKA with fully intact bodysides and the ZKA with the overloading cut-outs. When selecting your donor model, it pays to have a prototype example in mind as there are variations in the bodyside and end ribs depending on which builder fabricated the body.

With cheap and plentiful availability of the original POA/PNA releases, these have formed the basis for several Limpet conversions in miniature, cutting out the 5mm deep slots in the sides and adding plasticard bracing to complete. This could be considered unnecessary work when the required Limpet form is available RTR, but it is straightforward and saves a bit of money.

As one of Bachmann's oldest models, all versions of the wagon use the same chassis as under the TTA tanker, this dating from a time when the manufacturer did not cater for the full range of detail variations. Consequently, they all have the wrong

ABOVE: The Bachmann Limpet as supplied in Transrail and Loadhaul colours, these being fine to represent the wagons as running in the second half of the 1990s apart from correcting the suspension springs.

ABOVE: Bachmann has produced numerous POA/PNA models over the years, meaning they are readily available and often cheaper than buying actual Limpets. The side cut-outs can be made by milling out the plastic with a mini drill, tidying up the area with files and then adding styrene strip to make the extra ribs.

British Rail survivors

ABOVE: Also recoded as MKAs, two of the grey/yellow Limpets show off their weatherin, rust and distressed bodywork.

pattern of springs so the moulded leaf variant needs to be removed and replaced with the correct Bruninghaus pattern.

There are replacement whitemetal springs available from Stenson Models, now part of Will's Workbench, or S Kits but, on this occasion, a homemade 'bodge' was performed by slicing away the lower parts of the leaf springs with a scalpel and then attaching small pieces of plasticard towards the outer ends of the springs to give the correct look.

The tension lock couplings were also replaced with Smith's Instanter couplers, and this meant that the Bachmann NEM pockets could also be removed, opening up the space under the wagon. However, fitting Instanters or similar couplings to the Bachmann POA chassis can be challenging due to the dense volume of plastic in this area. A quick solution was to place the wagon upside down and drill a wide hole through the base of the wagon, approximately 3mm back from each bufferbeam. This then provides adequate space to easily install a coupling hook and secure the rear of it using superglue.

Staying underneath the chassis, the pair of heavy 'I' beams that run the length of the chassis are missing from the model so these can be replicated by adding styrene strip in the respective positions. Keen modellers may also wish to open out the holes in the chassis moulding where the W-irons join the underframe as well as fitting a depiction of the additional brake pipe runs, made from 0.3mm handrail wire. Further pieces of wire were used to replicate the connections between the brake shoes and also the U-shaped safety loops, all being bent to shape with pliers and superglued into the wagon floor.

Finishing

The Bachmann Limpets come alive once the livery elements are added, whether retaining the factory finish or conducting a full repaint. It is fun to replicate an exact prototype from a photograph, of which many can be found across the internet. Decals were sourced from Railtec, which has produced a dedicated sheet for the Limpets,

ABOVE: Work on the underframe can include adding the longitudinal beams as well as brake rods and safety loops, bringing some extra detail to what is otherwise a spartan chassis.

as well as various other sheets featuring wagon markings and data panels from both Railtec and Fox Transfers. These are always laid onto a gloss surface, so a coating of Railmatch gloss varnish was applied beforehand, and then finally a top coat of Railmatch matt varnish to seal in the decals before the weathering stages.

When it came to the weathering, each wagon firstly received a range of paint washes, which are designed to mute the original livery and build up the effect of dirt

ABOVE: With the white and light grey washes already applied, the Loadhaul Limpet is now receiving a brown wash, this including the white top capping.

in the sheltered areas around the ribs. On the Loadhaul example, washes of white and light grey were applied to tone down the bold black and orange, while on the other wagons, coatings of light brown enamel paints were applied and wiped away with kitchen towel and cotton buds.

The key when following this process is to work vertically downwards with each stroke of the cotton bud replicating how rainwater would move dirt down the bodysides. By building up several layers of browns, from light to dark, you can create a convincing finish of different colours. Next, individual blemishes and damage can be recreated using fine 5/0 paintbrushes. It is important to have brushes that end in a precise tip to aid applying

ABOVE: The Hobbycraft foamboard load formers are shown in place for test fitting prior to adding the Woodland Scenics ballast.

specific marks and following photos to ensure everything is applied in the correct location.

At this stage, each wagon was dry brushed with a larger paintbrush, dipped in brown and wiped almost entirely clean, which was run over the bodysides, with the paint landing just on the raised rib edges and highlighting the areas that are most susceptible to damage in real life. This action was repeated with several different shades of brown to build up a convincing rust effect.

The inside of the wagons were similarly painted with a palette of rusty tones before being filled with a spoil load. To save weight, Hobbycraft 5mm foamboard was used to pack out the bottom before topping off with a small amount of Woodland Scenics ballast, which is then secured in place with PVA glue. Small amounts of thinned paint can be dripped onto the load using a pipette, this settles into the load giving the look of oily, dirty ballast that has been removed from a worksite.

Each underframe was painted in a mottled range of browns and dark greys, again following photos to see where the oily moving parts were and using Humbrol Metalcote gunmetal to highlight exposed edges of the chassis. With weathering completed and loads installed, the final task was to apply a coat of Railmatch matt varnish to protect the wagons.

ABOVE: Transrail painted some of its Limpets into its plain grey livery but without any form of logo, these tending to have a more respectable finish than their sisters as a result.

Modelling BR: Engineers Wagons of Privatisation **25**

British Rail survivors

ZCA Sea Urchins

Continuing what BR started, Mainline, Transrail and EWS all rebuilt long-wheelbase air-braked wagons into ballast opens, creating a complex mishmash of designs. Simon Bendall attempts to unravel the story.

The Sea Urchin design first appeared in 1991 as BR looked to reduce its vacuum braked engineers' fleet by repurposing many of its surplus long-wheelbase air-braked open wagons and vans. As with so many conversions, the bodies were scrapped, and the chassis fitted with new low-sided bodywork to become ballast wagons.

Following the completion of a pair of prototypes, two batches of production rebuilds were authorised with an initial 43 OBAs being rebodied as ZCAs in 1991/92. A large batch of 400 conversions then followed in 1993 and early 1994, mostly using VDA vans as the donors but also some of the earlier VBAs. No matter the origin, all of these Sea Urchins were finished in grey/yellow.

Once the regional freight companies had been created and become established, both Mainline Freight and Transrail ordered further batches of rebuilds. For example, Mainline commissioned 70 conversions from RFS, Doncaster, in October 1995, for delivery from the following spring with 30 OAAs and 40 OBAs being rebuilt, and all finished in the company's blue livery. The two types looked very different though, the former OAAs having heavily ribbed bodywork while the ex OBAs had only five ribs and were largely identical to the BR conversions. Transrail also took 90 of the latter around the same period to the same design and finished in its grey livery with red capping.

EWS takes over

EWS wasted no time in adding more batches of Sea Urchins with RFS rebuilding 66 former VCA vans during 1997 while Crewe Works similarly tackled an initial 50 rebuilds of SPA, although the total eventually rose to 130. Both types were given heavily ribbed bodies but to different styles, the former SPAs having angled spill plates along their lower sides to prevent ballast lodging in place. In total across all batches, some 786 Sea Urchins were converted.

A handful of those rebuilt by BR, particularly from VBA and VDA vans, also received maroon repaints early in EWS ownership while others had ownership lettering added to their existing liveries. Following its takeover, all of the Sea Urchin batches worked together indiscriminately and also with the earlier ZCA Sea Horse and ZCA Sea Hare, making for highly colourful rakes containing an array of body designs.

However, the Sea Urchins were not a particularly efficient design as with a long wheelbase and only two wheelsets, axle loading limitations meant they could only carry around the same tonnage as the much shorter Coalfish. Over a comparable train length, this meant more Coalfish could be accommodated and more ballast moved compared to the Sea Urchins.

As a result, the mid-late 2000s saw all types of ZCA targeted for withdrawal with swathes sent for scrap during 2008. Some stragglers remained in use early into the next decade for specific duties, such as working with the RailVac machines and as internal barrier wagons at the Asfordby test track, but otherwise the Sea Urchins disappeared from traffic.

ABOVE: The Sea Urchins converted by BR in the early 1990s all passed to EWS ownership from 1996 and continued to operate as before with their engineers' grey/yellow colours becoming increasingly distressed. Converted from a VBA van in 1993/94, DC200639 became a ZCA(B) and is seen at Rugby in July 2000.

ABOVE: Large numbers of VDA vans were converted into Sea Urchins by BR, these being largely consistent in their appearance, although there were variations in the appearance of the ends for example. These retained the deeper 'fish-belly' underframes so were always easy to tell apart from other conversions. In EWS colours, ZCA(D) DC210205 was also at Rugby in July 2000.

British Rail survivors

ABOVE: The 40 Sea Urchin conversions conducted for Mainline Freight that used OBA opens as their donors followed the body style established by BR, having far fewer ribs. ZCA(P) M110289 arrives at Didcot in August 2001 finished in the company's blue livery.

ABOVE: Transrail also had 90 OBA opens converted into ZCA(P) Sea Urchins with the same bodywork, this design being the one portrayed by the 4mm scale Cambrian kit. Still in good condition, T110191 was part of a rake of seven such ZCAs arriving at Didcot in June 1999.

RIGHT: In contrast, the 30 OAA open wagons that became ZCA(O) for Mainline Freight all received heavily ribbed bodies in addition to blue paintwork. With such a small number converted, they were always something of a rarity in formations. M100067 arrives at Didcot from Eastleigh between two Transrail ZCA(P) in May 2000.

LEFT: When EWS sent former VCA vans for rebuilding in 1997, the resulting appearance mirrored that of the other van conversions. ZCA(C) DC200338 is shunted at Didcot in March 2001. The adjacent Shark ballast plough is noteworthy as being DB993711, one of the initial four dating from 1952 and built with bodywork to Oyster dimensions, which is a larger cabin, smaller verandas, and no doors. Having notched up 49 years of service, by this date it had been re-sheeted with plywood.

RIGHT: The last Sea Urchin conversions to appear utilised SPA plate wagons and derivatives as their basis. As shown by ZCA(Q) DC460998 at Rugby in July 2000, they had the most complex bodywork with angled surfaces to prevent ballast lodging on the ribs. The cut-outs around the bottom of the ribs were not universal, only appearing on around half of the 130 wagons converted. All photos Simon Bendall

Modelling BR: Engineers Wagons of Privatisation

British Rail survivors

ABOVE: The ex VDA Sea Urchins were relatively consistent in their appearance so the S Kits offering can be used for different batches. The BR era conversions lasted into the early 2000s in EWS ownership.

A mix of Urchins

Two kits exist in 4mm scale for different types of ZCA, both offering accurate routes to recreating the wagons. **Terry Bendall** builds both in mid-late 1990s condition.

Despite the number of different types of ZCA Sea Urchin, only one RTR model currently exists in OO gauge, this being the EFE Rail release from late last year. However, if you also consider kits, there are two long established options. The first from Cambrian Models dates from 2005 and builds one of the more numerous ex OBA designs while S Kits also offers a largely resin kit for the common ex VDA build.

Taking the latter first, this consists of a cast resin body, which includes the solebars, along with whitemetal ends, suspension, axleboxes and buffers. There are also etches for the W-irons, handbrake levers and steps. A departure from using the supplied parts was to employ the Stenson Models sprung W-iron kit (CC04S) since this includes the mountings for the brake disc callipers, which are very visible when viewed from the side.

The first job was to clean up the resin casting which, apart from removing the mould feed at one end, did not require a great deal of work. The whitemetal parts also needed only minimal preparation. One thing to check is that the ends are at 90 degrees to the sides using a small try square. With this addressed, the ends were put in place using superglue.

Chassis preparation

Attention then turned to the assembly of the Stenson suspension units. These are a bit fiddly in places so careful reading of the instructions is needed to get everything in the correct place and the various folds bent in the right direction. A trial fit of the suspension units between the resin solebars showed that they were too wide as the resin casting was fairly thick in the relevant places.

A lot of filing and scraping ensured to generate sufficient room but one of the consequences was that the resin became quite thin and fragile, and repairs had to be made using thin styrene strip cut to size. Some of the resin on the underside of the floor also had to be filed away. Although the instructions state that the wagon ends should be fitted before the suspension units are test fitted, this filing would have been a lot easier without them in place.

Once a satisfactory fit had been achieved, a transverse centre line was marked across the underside of the floor using a scriber and half the wheelbase length marked on each side. Transverse lines were then marked at the relevant positions to ensure the suspension units were glued on at right angles to the sides.

Suspension fitting

The Stenson suspension units allow the brass pinpoint bearings to move vertically in the slots of the W-irons so to achieve this, the holes in the cosmetic axle bearings also have to be made into slots to give clearance. This was done using a small rotary cutting tool held in a mini drill, although care is needed as this is a job where the bearing is likely to disappear into the far reaches of the workspace if caught by the burr! My method is to use a small block of wood with a hole drilled into the surface that the bearing will sit into and hold it with tweezers; this is not infallible, but it does help. Assembly of the sprung bearing carries and holding the bearing in the correct place is also helpful to make sure there is sufficient movement.

Once happy, the cosmetic bearings were glued in place and a further check made when the glue had set. More work with the cutting tool may be needed at this stage. All of this is best done before the suspension units are glued in place.

With the suspension units in and the glue set, the spring hangers and springs were glued in position and the bearing holders set up with the springs to make sure the suspension units functioned correctly. These were then removed to allow the brake rigging to be fixed. This is made from some fine brass etched parts, so care had to be taken not to lose any of the small items. There are different versions of the brake gear for these wagons so reference to pictures of the desired prototype is needed to ensure the correct parts are used and that they are fixed in the correct positions, both side of the wagon being different.

ABOVE: The inside of the ZCA kit first received a uniform spray of rust brown to serve as a base colour before browns and greys were dry brushed on. Shaking some loose ballast inside also leaves behind dust deposits.

British Rail survivors

ABOVE: **The Cambrian kit can be used for several ex OBA Sea Urchin batches, Mainline Freight having a number in its blue and yellow scheme.**

The brake gear was assembled using a combination of soldering and superglue, while footsteps were fitted to the right hand end of each side and some 0.3mm brass wire used to make the handrails. An air brake distributor and cylinder sourced from the spares box were fitted as were Roxey screw couplings and brake pipes scratchbuilt using 0.3mm and 0.45mm brass wire. The final touch was to fit some lamp brackets made from scrap brass etch.

Painting

Civil engineers' grey/yellow was chosen as the livery with the wagon first being sprayed in white, both to serve as an undercoat to check for imperfections and as a base coat for the yellow. Next, the yellow was added and then the Departmental grey, both having a touch of white mixed in to fade the colour. With the ex VDA Sea Urchins having a prominent angled rim along the sides, there is at least something to mask against but even so, with so many ribs to go over, paint runs are inevitable so some touching up was required to the joint between the yellow and grey. The solebars were painted last by hand and other colours picked out as needed.

Transfers mostly came from the old Appleby Model Engineering sheet intended for various ZCA varieties and these were subsequently varnished over. Weathering was largely done using dry brushing, paying particular attention to distressing the yellow, followed up by washes of brown shades over the sides and chassis. Internally, an all over rust colour had been sprayed on earlier and this was suitably distressed in the same way.

A plastic fish

Now 18 years old, Cambrian Models took an initial step towards fulfilling the need for Sea Urchins with this offering covering the ZCAs rebuilt from OBAs. The kit will either build the version with chamfered tops to the bodysides, as predominately converted by both Transrail and Mainline Freight in the mid-1990s, or with some body modifications, the earlier version with flat-topped sides rebuilt by BR from 1991 and finished in engineers' grey/yellow.

The contents of the kit will come as no surprise to anyone familiar with Cambrian's air-braked wagons, it consists of a five piece plastic body alongside the usual solebars, suspension units and other underframe parts widely used in other kits. Construction is straightforward with all of the parts a good fit and no particular problems were encountered.

Some of the smaller details are a little crude by today's standards, the buffers on the models pictured being replacements from MJT, while the brake equipment could also be upgraded with Stenson parts if desired. The Cambrian suspension units were also dispensed with in favour of etched W-irons to give reliable running and easy conversion to P4 gauge.

The Mainline Freight blue employed the Railmatch colour while the Transrail grey was a Humbrol grey deemed a good match upon comparison to photos. The red and yellow capping was similarly sourced with transfers, including the colour Transrail logos, coming from the discontinued Appleby range once again. Nowadays, Railtec offers the 'T' logos and has options for the number panels.

ABOVE: **The batch of Transrail-liveried ZCAs looked particularly striking when new, the red capping and coloured logo offsetting the grey nicely.**

ABOVE: **Based on the FTG Models SPA, the appearance of this batch of EWS conversions in RTR form as part of the OO gauge EFE Rail range in late 2022 was unexpected. Unfortunately, the model has a number of dimensional errors and general chunkiness that makes it something of a let-down. This is especially unfortunate as this batch of former SPAs had some of the more complex Sea Urchin bodywork, making them a challenge to scratchbuild.** Image courtesy Kernow Model Rail Centre

SELL YOUR P RAILWAY

Trade in with Hattons for payment within 1 or 2 days of your items arriving with us!

Use our self-service tools to list your collection quickly and easily online!

We purchase all manner of items:

- **LOCOS & ROLLING STOCK**
- **GARDEN RAILWAYS**
- **DIECAST VEHICLES**
- **UNBUILT PLASTIC KITS**

So why choose Hattons?

WE PAY STRAIGHT AWAY!*

- More than 70 years of experience
- Offering you the best prices in the industry
- Valuations made by experts
- Free quotes with no obligation to trade
- We can arrange delivery – no collection too big or too small
- Fast, secure payment • Store credit available

*Same day payments apply for collections received Monday to Friday before 2pm. Any collections received after 2pm will be paid on the next working day. Please note: In the unlikely event that we revise our offer price for your collection, you will be paid after responding to our offer. For full Terms and Conditions, visit hattons.co.uk/preownedterms

Get cash for your items in just four easy steps...

① List
Prepare & submit a list of your items online or send spreadsheets, documents or photographs to us via our website.

② Offer
Our expert staff will review your list and create your bespoke valuation.

③ Send
Once the offer is accepted, send your items to us.

④ Pay
Items are checked, the offer confirmed and payment made via **Bank Transfer, Cheque or PayPal**.

Start your trade in today at:

RE-OWNED MODEL ITEMS FOR CASH

GET A FREE VALUATION ON YOUR COLLECTION

We purchase a wide variety of brands, including...

The easiest way to put your list together...
Utilise our extensive product database and preset item conditions to quickly and easily compile your list.

 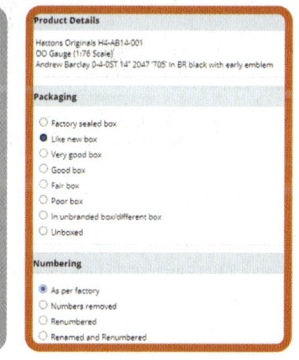

 Take our 60 second quiz and immediately learn if we can make an offer on your collection!
www.HattonsModelMoney.com/quiz

Get in touch with our friendly team...

Call us on: 0151 305 1755
Opening times: Mon to Sun 9:30am to 1pm / 2pm - 5pm

Email us at: preowned@hattons.co.uk

17 Montague Road, Widnes, WA8 8FZ

www.hattonsmodelmoney.com

Railtrack renewal

Railtrack renewal

With the arrival of new owners for the infrastructure and rolling stock, a review of the operation of track renewal trains brought a substantial reorganisation of how things were done. Simon Bendall looks at the changes that were introduced.

ABOVE: The new look for infrastructure services following investment by both Railtrack and EWS is demonstrated by 66167 as it nears Stoneycombe on September 28, 2002, with the 6G86 14.15 Exeter Riverside to St Blazey. This is formed of a set of recently converted JJA autoballasters, but the following month would see Railtrack replaced by Network Rail. *Trevor Mann Collection*

As privatisation took effect, Railtrack and EWS inherited an out-dated method of running infrastructure services as well as locos that were unreliable and wagons that were inefficient. A comparison to Foster Yeoman showed that the private freight operator was able to move 1,500 tonnes of aggregates at a time, whereas the average ballast train could manage just 400 tonnes. As a result, more trains were running in order to move the same tonnage, requiring more rolling stock resources.

The two companies jointly conducted a fundamental review to see what improvements could be made, resulting in a number of changes, including the creation of the National Logistics Unit to oversee movements, materials procurement, and asset management. A central element of the new policy was the creation of the virtual quarries, where ballast from quarries could be stockpiled at strategic locations across the network to await use. This meant it could be moved in bulk quantities rather than BR's policy of constantly sending comparatively low-capacity ballast trains to the quarries for refilling, saving time, money, and mileage.

In addition, Local Distribution Centres (LDCs) were established where trains for possession work would be formed up in advance. This allowed the number of locations used for such work to be slashed from 44 to 16 by 2001 and served as stockpiling sites for all the materials needed for renewal work. Railtrack encouraged its various maintenance contractors to also establish operating bases at the same locations to give further integration.

Sleepers and rail

In the early years of privatisation, concrete sleepers were supplied by the RMC plant at Washwood Heath and Tarmac's works at Tallington, near Peterborough. When the introduction of steel sleepers came for lightly used routes, these were manufactured by Corus as well as being imported from America. With the subsequent closure of the RMC plant, a new sleeper production centre was constructed by Network Rail and its partners at Doncaster, this opening in February 2014 with a capability of manufacturing 400,000 concrete sleepers a year.

Network Rail also expanded the number of suppliers for rail beyond the traditional source of Workington and later Scunthorpe, contracting firms in Italy and Austria to deliver rails, these reaching the UK by ship or through the Channel Tunnel. Welding of rail lengths to form continuous welded rail still takes place today at Scunthorpe and Eastleigh.

Recycling

Once the renewal aspect of track maintenance had been recast, attention then turned to the other side of the operation, how best to dispose of redundant materials. In a process started by Railtrack and continued by Network Rail, sections of LDCs were configured to function as reception points for redundant sleepers, rails, ballast, and other materials.

By the early 2000s, some 95% of spent ballast was being recycled, much of it being sold off for use in the foundations of building sites or roads. Scrap rail was cut into short lengths and sent to steelworks to be melted down while wooden sleepers were sold off to the burgeoning landscaping sector. However, changes to environmental regulations from 2003 saw creosoted sleepers classified as hazardous, these instead being sent to an Energy from Waste plant to be burned to generate electricity.

In more recent years, Network Rail has established even larger recycling centres at the likes of Whitemoor, Hoo Junction, Basford Hall, and Westbury to process materials with large amounts of ballast now sent to the reactivated sidings at Longport, Stoke, from across northern England for reprocessing, these workings being carried out by Land Recovery with Colas as the haulier.

Railtrack renewal

LEFT: Another of Railtrack's new wagon fleets is seen in action at Markshall, near Norwich, on February 24, 2002, as a MRA side tipper shows off its capabilities in front of assembled trackworkers. The ballast would be used to form the track-bed. In the background, GB Railfreight's 66706 stands at the head of the train. Tim Horn

RIGHT: Road-rail machinery has become a key part of track renewals during the privatisation era, performing many of the functions for which specialist rail vehicles were previously converted. On April 8, 2018, a grab from TXM Plant tidies up the worksite at Longforgan following track replacement. OBA 110312 is bringing up the rear of the 6K14 Millerhill to Barnhill. Jim Ramsay

LEFT: All the trappings of a modern worksite can be seen at Balmossie on March 10, 2019, as new concrete sleepers await the installation of new continuous welded rail. OCAs 112321 and 112172 are in the process of being loaded with the timber spacers used to separate the stacks of concrete sleepers brought in on the Salmons and FEA flats making up the rest of the train. Jim Ramsay

Modelling BR: Engineers Wagons of Privatisation

Railtrack renewal

The virtual quarries

Introduced by Railtrack, the concept of stockpiling ballast at major infrastructure yards rather than continually having to visit quarries was a simple solution to more efficient train operation. David Ratcliffe looks at their development over the years.

Following privatisation, Railtrack in collaboration with its major engineering contractors undertook a review of infrastructure services with the aim of creating operating efficiencies. As a result, 1996 saw 16 Local Distribution Centres (LDCs) created, where possession trains were to be marshalled, along with 14 Virtual Quarries (VQs), where large stockpiles of new ballast were to be kept. These were all established at strategic locations across the network with, if possible, a virtual quarry at the same site as an LDC.

In northwest England, both Carnforth and Guide Bridge became small VQs, with Guide Bridge also acting as an LDC, but this arrangement was soon replaced by the opening of a much larger combined facility at Crewe Basford Hall. Meanwhile in Scotland, both Millerhill and Mossend were designated as LDCs while the virtual quarry was located at Carstairs, which received its stone by road from the nearby Cloburn Quarry.

A further change to its operations, which Railtrack introduced in 1997, was to reduce the number of quarries which supplied it with ballast from over a dozen to just six. Those that remained were Cloburn, Penmaenmawr, Machen, Mountsorrel, Stud Farm, and Glensanda, with the stone from Glensanda being shipped directly to the virtual quarries that were set up on the coast at Grain, Purfleet, and Southampton.

Some of the Glensanda stone that was landed at Southampton Docks was then moved by rail to the virtual quarry at Westbury, while other block ballast workings were introduced to serve the rest of the virtual quarries. From Penmaenmawr in North Wales, trains ran to Carnforth and Guide Bridge, and later Crewe, while Stud Farm supplied the virtual quarries set up at Bescot, Rugby and Oxford Hinksey.

The busiest of the originating points was Mountsorrel, from where bulk ballast trains ran to the VQs at Doncaster, Peterborough, Toton, and Tyne Yard, while in subsequent years Mountsorrel has also supplied the newer VQs that have opened at Carlisle, Crewe, Derby Chaddesden Sidings, and March Whitemoor. In Wales, no virtual quarry was provided with a service from Machen Quarry instead working to the LDC at Newport.

ABOVE: The EWS duo of 37375 and 37042 disturb the peace as they slog up the 1 in 70 gradient approaching Upton Scudamore on February 27, 2002, while working the 6Z86 14.30 Westbury Yard to Eastleigh virtual quarry loaded ballast, this being a short term flow that had originated from Meldon Quarry in Devon. Although the rundown of the English Electric machines was well underway by this point, 37375 still had two years left to run with its sister lasting longer still, until January 2005. The wagons are a uniform rake of JRA boxes owned by GE Rail Services, which had acquired Tiphook. In 4mm, this is available as a resin kit from S Kits. Mark Few

Wagons

Until privatisation, infrastructure trains had been the poor relations of the freight scene, often being reliant on elderly cast-off wagons that were no longer required by the revenue fleet. However, with such services now run on a contractual basis and infrastructure traffic established as a commercial business, there was a priority to modernise and rationalise the wagon fleet.

To handle the bulk ballast workings to virtual quarries, which amounted to around two million tonnes a year, Railtrack invested in a fleet of 120 new JNA 102-tonne GLW high-sided bogie box wagons. These were built by Marcroft Engineering, Stoke, during 1998 and had a capacity of 78

LEFT: Oxford Hinksey Yard is home to one of the more compact virtual quarries, a single line serving the ballast stockpile. In less than ideal conditions, a rake of Railtrack JNAs is unloaded by the resident grab in 1999. The withdrawn overhead line maintenance coaches and parcels vans alongside were provided as a makeshift acoustic barrier due to complaints by nearby residents until a large wooden fence was constructed. Simon Bendall

Railtrack renewal

ABOVE: **To supplement its own fleet of wagons, Railtrack leased a number of bogie boxes for its virtual quarry traffic. Originally built for Channel Tunnel segment traffic, KEA PR3276 was recorded laying over for the weekend in Didcot Yard in August 2000 while working to Hinksey. Again, S Kits produces this as resin kit in 4mm.** Simon Bendall

ABOVE: **Another type to see brief use carrying ballast were the former British Steel South Wales iron ore boxes which were purchased by VTG in 2003. With its lettering crudely painted over, JTA VTG26676 was at Crewe Gresty Lane in January 2005. Revolution Trains and Accurascale are the source of models in N and OO.** David Ratcliffe

tonnes. Leased from Caib and numbered CAIB3400-3519, the JNAs were finished in a distinctive green livery with large boards on the side lettered 'Railtrack Renewing your Railway'.

These vehicles were initially introduced on the service from Penmaenmawr Quarry to Guide Bridge, with a 20 wagon train running two or three times a week, while to supplement the JNAs, Railtrack also ordered a batch of two-axle low-sided box wagons suitable for both ballast and spoil traffic. Coded PNA and numbered CAIB3600-3849, these wagons first appeared on the service from Penmaenmawr to Carnforth but, like the JNAs, were soon seen working more widely.

In addition to its own fleet, Railtrack also leased some high-sided bogie boxes from the wagon hirers Tiphook and VTG. However, these wagons were not ideal for infrastructure use since if they strayed into spoil traffic, they were easily prone to being overloaded.

A rather more innovative wagon design that saw some use in the movement of new ballast to virtual quarries were the Redland/Lafarge Self-Discharge Trains based at Mountsorrel. While usually occupied in carrying stone to the company's own distribution depots in East Anglia and southern England, the SDTs would occasionally deliver ballast to either Doncaster or Whitemoor.

By 2004, investment in new infrastructure wagons had gathered even more pace for, in addition to the new MRA side-tipping wagons, Network Rail was also taking delivery of new JNA Falcon 90-tonne GLW bogie box wagons. With lower sides than the earlier Railtrack JNAs, these vehicles were intended for both ballast and spoil traffic to and from possessions but, for several years, they could also be found working between quarries and virtual quarries.

Five years later in 2009, Network Rail also received a batch of 120 new 102-tonne GLW high-sided bogie box wagons. TOPS coded IOA and given the codename of Mussel, these wagons soon took over the majority of the bulk ballast movements to the virtual quarries.

However, in recent years, even this fleet has been insufficient to meet demand and from 2018 an increasing number of MRAs, which had been designed for use in dropping ballast at relaying sites, were transferred to the bulk ballast flows. This development saw the generator set fitted to some of the MRAs either removed or disabled. Most recently, Network Rail has leased a further 50 new high-sided bogie box wagons from Wascosa, these JNA joining the earlier IOAs on bulk ballast deliveries to virtual quarries.

ABOVE: **The Network Rail infrastructure contracts are a major source of income for the freight operators and demand the best resources available, a far cry from BR days. On August 3, 2016, 68017 *Hornet* was in charge of a diverted 6Z77 13.58 Mountsorrel-Crewe Basford Hall as it passes Cossington on the Midland Main Line. The DRS working was running via Leicester due to a bridge collapse at Barrow upon Soar and featured 20 loaded IOAs.** Paul Biggs

Modelling BR: Engineers Wagons of Privatisation **35**

Railtrack renewal

ABOVE: Crewe Basford Hall has become a major centre for Network Rail infrastructure traffic over the years, its location providing a base for operations in the northwest along with north and mid Wales. A virtual quarry nestles in part of the marshalling yard, adjacent to the West Coast Main Line and next to Freightliner's loco fuelling point. On August 27, 2018, 66768 passes by with the Clitheroe-Avonmouth cement tanks while a rake of IOA ballast boxes from Mountsorrel has been split into two halves for unloading. Rob Higgins

ABOVE: With only limited space at Basford Hall, the sidings at Crewe Gresty Lane have also been given over to infrastructure use, serving principally as a maintenance base for a high-output ballast train. Additional stabling space is also available for wagons and track machines as seen on September 29, 2018, as a Freightliner Class 66 passes with Salmons loaded with track panels and fresh ballast in JNA Falcons and MLAs. Rob Higgins

Railtrack renewal

ABOVE: With Newcastle forming the skyline, DB Cargo's 66109 in its unique PD Ports blue livery passes Tyne Yard with the 4E96 Mossend-Tees Dock intermodal. Much of the complex has been repurposed for infrastructure use with a relatively compact virtual quarry existing alongside another maintenance depot for high-output ballast equipment. *Rob Higgins*

ABOVE: The virtual quarry at Bescot is squeezed onto the former loco holding sidings, with the marshalling yard and Bescot Stadium station on one side and the River Tame and the M6 on the other. On September 2, 2018, 66422 arrives in the up yard with the daily Crewe-Toton infrastructure service which calls at Bescot to drop off and pick up wagons. The consist on this day was Colas and Volker Rail Kirow cranes. *Rob Higgins*

Modelling BR: Engineers Wagons of Privatisation 37

Railtrack renewal

JNA ballast boxes

Railtrack's first significant investment in wagons was for its virtual quarries project and it included leasing a fleet of newly built bogie boxes. Simon Bendall looks at their history while Mike Cubberley tackles a resin kit in OO gauge.

ABOVE: Riding on English Steel ESC1 bogies with clasp brakes, a brand new CAIB3418 is seen at Guide Bridge virtual quarry in September 1998, the month it entered service. David Ratcliffe

The summer of 1998 saw Marcroft Engineering hard at work at its Stoke workshops constructing the first of a fleet of 102-tonne gross laden weight JNA bogie boxes for bulk ballast flows to the new virtual quarries. These were to be owned by Caib and leased to Railtrack, the whole fleet emerging in the infrastructure owner's new green livery with large nameboards proclaiming 'Railtrack Renewing Your Railway' in silver.

While the boxes were new, their bogies were not, being a mix of ESC and Gloucester types recovered from scrapped tank wagons and bogie presflos as was the brake equipment. Construction started at CAIB3400 and went up, as well as CAIB3519 going down, the two series meeting in the middle during the spring of 1999 with 120 examples built.

The first batch had entered service the previous September with CAIB3400-19 running to Penmaenmawr to commence the distribution of ballast across the northwest, such as to Ashburys in Manchester. As more were delivered, the JNAs spread to other routes, for example working from Mountsorrel to Toton and Hinksey. A notable oddity among the fleet was CAIB3469, which was delivered fitted with Powell Duffryn LTF25 low track force bogies. As a result, it spent the early months of its career based at Derby undergoing performance trials.

The use of this batch of JNAs for virtual quarry duties was quite short-lived, being handed back soon after Network Rail took over from Railtrack. They subsequently lost their nameboards and were redeployed onto a variety of aggregates and scrap metal flows, passing to VTG ownership when it acquired Caib. This brought structural alterations, most notably the fitting of an access hatch on each side and modifications to the corners of the box body. At some point, CAIB3469 also lost its experimental bogies.

ABOVE: Fitted with disc-braked Gloucester bogies, CAIB3481 was already well used when recorded at Warrington Arpley in May 1999. Following acquisition by VTG, the ownership prefix on the number was suitably amended. David Ratcliffe

Railtrack renewal

ABOVE: With three Railtrack PNAs and seven JNAs in the formation, 37379 *Ipswich WRD Quality Assured* was recorded shunting Chaddesden Yard, Derby, on March 30, 2001. It would later depart with the empty wagons as the 6T21 16.03 working to Toton. *Phil Chilton*

RIGHT: With the use of secondhand bogies, brake gear and buffers, there was quite some variation to be found across the 120 wagons. CAIB3460 was another to be mounted on ESC1 bogies when also recorded at Arpley in May 1999. *David Ratcliffe*

Building an S Kits JNA

This is an S Kits resin and whitemetal kit which builds this batch of JNAs as they were in Railtrack use before the alterations to the bodywork.

Construction began by trimming off any excess resin, filling any 'blow holes' and bubble marks, and then fettling the main body sections. Holes for the handrails and buffers were also drilled out, with the former added using the supplied nickel silver wire. Once the adhesive had dried fully on these, any excess wire poking through on the inside of the body was trimmed back flush with the sides as far as possible.

Construction of the body started by adding one end to a side, with the floor following next and then the other side and end. The squareness of the body was checked at each stage of its construction, with any removal of resin achieved by careful use of a large file. A bead of glue was also added all around the floor to body joints to give extra strength.

The whitemetal bogies had the bearing holes carefully opened out to the required depth and width with 2mm brass bearings then added. The bogies were assembled using a rapid set epoxy glue, although soldering is also an option if you feel you have asbestos fingers!

The bodyside nameboards for the Railtrack lettering were added from five thou styrene sheet and attached with some light dabs of superglue. They had to be made slightly longer than specified in the instructions to fit correctly across the ribs. Finally, the buffers and brake equipment were put in place.

After a wash and scrub with an old toothbrush and creme cleaner, the body was given some grey primer from an aerosol can and then Halfords Rover Green was sprayed on. This was the nearest currently available aerosol colour that I could find, although Freightliner green is also a reasonable match.

Once fully dried after a couple of days, Railtec transfers (sheet No. 6482) were added along with some assorted Fox decals to give some of the additional data and overhead warning markings. The bogies were cleaned up with some white spirit and then painted with two coats of Games Workshop 'Abaddon Black' acrylic paint and the axleboxes picked out with Railmatch warning yellow acrylic.

The body was finally given a couple of light coats of Army Painter flat matt varnish. The last touches included adding the couplings and brake pipes from the spares box while a black and rusty brown acrylic paint mix was used on the inside of the body to complete the model.

ABOVE: The OO gauge S Kits resin offering is the only available model of the Railtrack JNAs in any scale, it being one of a number of such box wagons offered by the manufacturer.

Railtrack renewal

PNA ballast opens

Built concurrently with the JNAs were a fleet of two-axle PNA wagons also for use by Railtrack, these used an array of recovered underframes as their basis. Simon Bendall again looks at their evolution while Mike Cubberley splices together two 4mm Bachmann models to produce a pedestal suspension variant.

ABOVE: CAIB3787 was built using the underframe of Ribble Cement PCA presflo RBL10436, it has a five-rib body, ESC pedestal suspension and a handbrake level. It is seen at Warrington in February 2000. *David Ratcliffe*

In addition to the JNA bogie boxes, Railtrack also procured a fleet of two-axle low-sided box wagons, again for virtual quarry work, although hey did also appear in other infrastructure services mixed in with EWS' Coalfish family and other types. These were once more leased from Caib and built by Marcroft Engineering at Stoke, being coded PNA. Construction began shortly after the JNAs in the late summer of 1998 with the first examples released to traffic that November, the debut workings again being from Penmaenmawr. By the end of the year, some 60 examples were in traffic, which had risen to just over 200 in April 1999 with the eventual fleet total being 250.

Like their bigger cousins, the PNAs married new box bodies with second-hand underframes, these came from a variety of sources and resulted in a host of detail differences across the build. For CAIB3600 to CAIB3749, the underframes from various batches of TTA tankers were employed, these all being of 'traditional' design with handbrake levers, W-irons and Bruninghaus springs. However, for CAIB3750 to CAIB3849, the chassis were taken from more modern donors, either TUA tankers or PCA cement presflos. As a result, these featured a mix of ESC or Gloucester pedestal suspension and typically had a wheelbase that was around a foot longer. There was also a mix of handbrake levers or wheels. Further variation was found in the design of the bodies on all batches with some having five bodyside ribs and others seven. One common aspect was that they were all finished in Railtrack green with the silver 'Railtrack Renewing Your Railway' branding, but even the positioning of this varied due to spacing differences in the ribs!

The PNA fleet continued in traffic throughout the decade, acquiring the paper codename of Piranha and becoming increasingly dirty and dishevelled with the Railtrack lettering disappearing under the grime. With ownership passing to VTG, the number prefix began to be altered accordingly from August 2008 but with the arrival of the IOA boxes the following year, all 250 wagons were taken off lease and stored at Long Marston.

This was the end of the line for CAIB3600-3749, their elderly chassis counting against them, and all were duly disposed of for scrap. However, around ten of those with pedestal suspension saw further use from the autumn of 2013 when they were leased by DC Rail for use with the first of the RailVacs, the freight company having secured the haulage contract for the giant vacuum machine. The PNAs were formed either side of it to carry fresh ballast and receive the spent ballast, this arrangement continuing for around a year until the contract was taken over by Colas and the PNAs replaced by Coalfish and Falcons. Thereafter, they joined their sisters in going for scrap.

ABOVE: Based on numerous visits to Didcot in the early 2000s, the Railtrack PNAs were a rarity in the area, only turning up every so often when compared to their EWS equivalents. However, in April 2001, five-rib CAIB3695 was part of a small number mixed in with Coalfish. This employed the chassis of TTA BRT57733 so has Bruninghaus springs and conventional W-irons. *Simon Bendall*

ABOVE: Recorded at Crewe Gresty Lane in July 2002, CAIB3828 illustrates one of the PNAs with a seven-rib body. This used the chassis from TUA PR70161 so has Gloucester pedestal suspension, handbrake wheels and a largely bare underframe with a longer wheelbase. *David Ratcliffe*

Railtrack renewal

RIGHT: Built on the frame of TTA BRT57598, CAIB3648 arrives at Didcot behind 58002 *Daw Mill Colliery* in the summer of 2000. The real interest is provided by ZXW DB904697 which is carrying Jarvis-owned Donelli single line track relaying gantry 78417. Behind is sister Lowmac DB904709 with 78416 and, out of sight, former Mk.1 carflat YRW DB745229 with their accompanying lifting beam. As their TOPS codes would suggest, the trio are vacuum-braked vehicles with a through air pipe so were running unfitted with a long string of Sea Urchins behind. Simon Bendall

LEFT: Now re-prefixed, VTG3612 is seen in store at Long Marston on August 8, 2010, showing the condition the PNAs were in after leaving Network Rail service. This is a seven-rib body on a former TTA chassis, in this case from former Shell tanker SUKO67147. Simon Bendall

Building a pedestal PNA

This model is an amalgamation of two mostly Bachmann ready-to-run models in order to create one of the Railtrack PNAs fitted with pedestal suspension, these being otherwise unavailable in model form. By combining the body of the five-ribbed PNA model with the chassis from the POA/SSA scrap wagon, it provides a close representation of the pedestal type without resorting to scratchbuilding the whole wagon.

Bachmann's PNA is of the wagons built on a TTA tanker chassis with conventional suspension, so this underframe needs to be removed and placed in the spares box. The same is true of the SSA but this time it is the body that is put in the parts donor pile. The donor chassis is longer than the body it will be going under so some surgery is required.

Taking the two parts, it is best to line up the solebar/body support plates with the bodyside ribs centrally and then use a razor saw to cut away the excess chassis length plus the width of the bufferbeams. The mountings for the handbrake wheels also need to be removed at this stage and the air brake distributor and reservoir recovered from the SSA donor body. The representations of the disc brake hangers that are inboard of the suspension units also need to go but are worth placing in the spares box.

The chassis is then stuck onto the body and the bufferbeams re-attached. Once it is all set, filler should be applied to the chassis sections to help hide the cuts. New handbrake lever supports were made from 20 thou styrene sheet profiled with a file and attached to the chassis. The actual handbrake levers came from a Cambrian SSA kit and were extended in length with a strip of 10 thou styrene. These were then secured with a light application of superglue to minimise drying time while bending the extension strip around the springs and axlebox moulding to achieve the correct shape for the levers.

RIGHT: Combining the PNA body and SSA chassis gives a good representation of the pedestal suspension wagons and brings some welcome variety to a train.

Fitting couplings of your choice can then take place, along with mounting the brake distributor and reservoir under the body. The last three digits of the printed wagon number were carefully removed with a curved knife blade and replaced with transfers from a Fox sheet. Finally, the bright blue former SSA chassis was painted black.

ABOVE: Like the ZKA Limpet, Bachmann's model of the PNAs has incorrect leaf springs rather than Bruninghaus due to it using the one size fits all TTA chassis. The springs can be carved off and replaced with the correct type available from Stenson Models or S Kits. The Stenson replacements are shown in place but prior to painting to show the work required with the modifications described in full in the MTA section on pages 48-49. Bachmann's initial releases of the PNAs, of which this is one, incorrectly added a plural to 'Railway' so this needs correcting, either that or purchase later batches which were amended.

Modelling BR: Engineers Wagons of Privatisation

MFA ballast wagons

Dating from 2000, the cut-down MEA boxes have served in ballast and spoil trains for over two decades. Simon Bendall looks at their history and the models available.

The arrival of the new Thrall-built MBA 'monster box' wagons from 1999 left EWS with a surplus of its much-smaller two-axle MEA box wagons. Initially developed by Railfreight Coal a decade earlier, the MEAs were created by placing a sturdy high-sided box body on chassis reclaimed from scrapped HEA domestic coal hoppers. With the coming of privatisation, further batches were ordered by both Mainline Freight and Loadhaul as the MEAs were suitable for a range of bulk aggregates in addition to coal, something that EWS recognised by commissioning additional conversions.

However, the small size of the MEAs compared unfavourably with higher-capacity bogie boxes so it was no surprise that they were increasingly deemed surplus as the MBAs rolled out. However, with the bodies still having plenty of life in them and a number of vacuum-braked ballast opens still in traffic, particularly the Clams, it was a straightforward decision to repurpose a number of MEAs as ballast wagons.

This was achieved by cutting down the bodywork to around half its original height, creating low-sided boxes that were suitable for both ballast and spoil work, a process that commenced at both Wabtec, Doncaster,

ABOVE: Still fresh from conversion, 391102 shows off its patch-painted Mainline Freight blue livery at Didcot in March 2001. Rebuilt at Marcroft, the bottom of the body has been cut away, reunited with its floor, and then welded back onto the chassis, with the paintwork retouched in a slightly different shade of blue all around. The logo and number panels have also been fully repainted. Simon Bendall

and Marcroft, Stoke, in the summer of 2000. The resulting wagons were recoded as MFA but retained both their existing numbers and liveries, although gold EWS lettering was added centrally on the sides.

ABOVE: Only six of the Loadhaul batch of MEAs were cut down to create MFAs so were a rarity compared to the other liveries. Also fresh from conversion, 391223 was at Didcot in February 2001 sandwiched between an MTA and another MFA, the two types working alongside each other for 22 years. Loadhaul's MEAs never carried any orange, unlike many of the company's other repainted wagons, so neither did the MFA conversions. Simon Bendall

ABOVE: The Wabtec method of rebuilding is illustrated by 391049 at Didcot in the same month, it has had the top of its body removed and then new capping added. As a result, the fresh grey and yellow paint is around the top of the box rather than the bottom, allowing the Railfreight Coal logo to still be carried. Many of the early MFA withdrawals came from the ex Railfreight batch, presumably as their bodies were somewhat older than the later conversions. Simon Bendall

Railtrack renewal

MFA ballast wagons
Railfreight Coal grey/yellow: 391001/06/17/25/27/34/46-82
Mainline Freight blue: 391101/02/05/09/11/27/29/31/37/38/43-46
Loadhaul black: 391205/22/23/27/35/36
EWS maroon: 391246/48/49/52/57/58/63/65/71/72/78/79/87/88/91/92, 391302/03/16/31/46/49/53/57/64/68/72/80/81/86/96, 391402/04/05/08/12/14/16/18/20/24/30/36/42/44/45/47/51/62/69/82/83/87/93/94, 391508-10/23/30/33/44/45/47/62/72/77/81/91/93, 391613/17

Upper or lower

Notably, the two workshops involved went about the work in different ways with Wabtec simply cutting down the top of the bodies and replacing the capping. Marcroft instead opted to remove each box from its underframe, cut away the lower metalwork and then remount the body. In both cases, the paintwork was made good with a partial repaint using whatever livery colour the wagon was already in. It was therefore easy to tell where each MFA had been converted as they either had fresh grey, blue, black, or maroon at the top or bottom of the bodies! By the time conversions were concluded late in 2000, 135 MFAs had been created with the table detailing their identities and the liveries carried upon conversion.

The MFAs were allocated to nationwide usage, soon finding their way to all areas of the country and working alongside the likes of the MHAs. They have subsequently led unremarkable lives but a limited amount of repaints have enlivened things. As early as 2006, some of those that retained Railfreight grey upon conversion were observed with fresh maroon on the sides but still retaining yellow ends, examples including 391001, 391006 and 391027. Much more noticeable was the complete repaint of 391034 into DB Cargo red at Stoke, when it emerged in the yard at the wagon works in March 2016. However, here it remained for the next 14 months until it was finally released to traffic in May 2017.

The liveries of the MFA subsequently degenerated into the usual mix of rust and dirt, making the underlying colour hard to determine, although when the EWS lettering was painted out around 2015, this brought a patch of fresh maroon in many cases. Withdrawals commenced in the late-2010s prompted by the arrival of the MXA Lobsters and have remained a steady trickle ever since, although examples were still in traffic in April 2023.

ABOVE: An already work-stained 391572 is seen stabled in Hinksey Yard in April 2001 with a load of spoil while flanked by an MTA and MHA 394311. Mixed rakes of the three types were common for a time in the early 2000s until the braking characteristics of the MTAs brought restrictions on how they were marshalled. Simon Bendall

ABOVE: Only one MFA has received DB red to date and, in all probability given the type's ongoing reduction, 391034 will remain unique. Although completed in 2016, it was not released into traffic for over a year and is seen engaged on a possession at Inchture level crossing, to the west of Dundee, on April 14, 2018. Despite the paintjob, it was sent for scrap in January 2022. Jim Ramsay

Bachmann MFA models

Bachmann was relatively quick to release the MFA in OO gauge, it being a simple re-use of the existing HEA/MEA chassis with a newly tooled body. All four liveries of Railfreight Coal, Mainline Freight, Loadhaul and EWS were issued together and there have been periodic re-runs ever since. More recent models are the ones to go for where possible though as these feature the re-tooled HEA chassis, which has much finer handbrake levers and other enhancements. The MFA has similarly featured in the manufacturer's Graham Farish range, albeit less frequently. Neither scale has yet seen the DB-liveried wagon, but it will doubtless be along in due course.

LEFT: The initial releases of the Bachmann MFA included 391102 in Mainline blue and 391070 in Railfreight Coal, the first of these being based on the photo at the top of the opposite page.

RIGHT: The other two models to be released first were EWS maroon 391572 and Loadhaul black 391223.

LEFT: The N gauge Farish MFA is perhaps a bit on the chunky side, this being the EWS-liveried release of, once again, 391572. Picture courtesy of Hattons

Modelling BR: Engineers Wagons of Privatisation

Railtrack renewal

MHA/MPA ballast wagons

Known as Coalfish, these are the most numerous of the EWS/DB two-axle boxes, being built on the underframes of HAA coal hoppers. Having served for 25 years, they are now in decline as **Simon Bendall** details.

With a considerable number of vacuum-braked ballast wagons to eliminate, EWS placed its first contract for a new fleet of rebodied low-sided boxes with RFS in the spring of 1997. Coded MHA, an initial 125 HAA merry-go-round coal hoppers and derivatives would see their bodies scrapped and the chassis reused under the heavily ribbed bodies, although the number to be rebuilt was soon increased to 400.

By that August, over 50 had been released into traffic from Doncaster, all carrying EWS maroon with yellow capping and numbered from 394001 upwards. These were initially deployed to the West Coast Main Line but as more MHAs were outshopped, they quickly spread to other routes. The wagons soon acquired the codename of Coalfish and in a rarity for the privatisation era, this was physically applied to the solebars of all wagons between 394069 and 394203 with the exception of 394071-074/079-084 and 394201/202. All 400 MHA had been completed by the end of 1998 with 394400 being the last.

It was not until late 2001 that more MHA conversions appeared, the small batch of five wagons being created by cutting down the prototype MAA coal boxes. These had been rebuilt in 1988/89 by fitting new high-sided box bodies to HAA hopper chassis as an initial trial for replacing the remaining vacuum-braked mineral wagons in South Wales. While the decision was eventually taken to turn HEA hoppers into MEA coal boxes instead, the quintet of MAAs remained in service alongside them.

However, with the arrival of the MBA 'monster boxes', they were available for conversion and duly reduced in height, being renumbered as 394406-10. As they were

ABOVE: **The look of the original 16-rib MHA Coalfish conversions is typified by 394369 at Didcot in the summer of 2000. The use of the HAA chassis meant they retained the unusual mix of clasp and disc brakes.** Simon Bendall

merely cut down rather than rebodied, all five retained their Railfreight grey livery with yellow ends and, in some cases, the Coal sub-sector emblems.

Revised design
From the spring of 2002, another large batch of MHA conversions got underway at what was now Wabtec, Doncaster, with fabricated bodies also sent by road to the wagon repair depot at Margam to be fitted to additional wagons there. The introduction of the Thrall-built HTA coal hoppers had released further members of the HAA family for conversion

ABOVE: **The Coalfish branding given to around 120 of the first wave of conversions is displayed by 394144 at Bardon Hill Quarry on July 18, 1998. This was one of several MHAs present that had been loaded with large granite boulders for transport to Hessle.** David Ratcliffe

ABOVE: **The five MAA boxes retained their Railfreight sub-sector colours upon conversion to Coalfish, 394410 being captured at Chaddesden Sidings in May 2001. Like the MFAs, they received a partial repaint all round to cover the new metalwork.** Mark Saunders

Railtrack renewal

ABOVE: Seen at South Kenton on July 31, 2007, 394597 demonstrates the revised style of bodywork introduced from 394500 with only 11 bodyside ribs. Timara Easter

ABOVE: Only one MHA received a full repaint in DB red, 11-rib 394829 being completed at Stoke in March 2016 and then stored for 14 months in the same manner as solitary MFA 391034. On August 11, 2017, it was already turning pink when recorded at Hoo Junction. Dan Adkins

with the remaining MGV/ZCV Clams initially targeted for replacement.

However, these conversions differed from the previous batch by only having 11 bodyside ribs instead of the original 16, creating quite a different look to the bodies with larger panels in between. Numbering commenced from 394500 and climbed ever upwards during the 2000s as further batches were added on. When 394999 was reached, the number series jumped to 396000 as the MTAs were occupying the 395xxx series.

The MHA conversions finally concluded with 396165 in the spring of 2007, some of the last rebuilds having taken place at Stoke. All of the wagons were once again finished in EWS maroon and with such a huge number available were to be found in every corner of the country carrying ballast, spoil, sand and recovered sleepers.

Late in 2016, some Coalfish began to be recoded as MPA, this denoting wagons where the brake discs were an integral part of the wheel faces, rather than being separate steel plates bolted on. Wagons with the latter style remained coded MHA and also in the majority but the MPA recodes spread quite widely across all Coalfish batches and number series, including two of the former MAAs.

Despite the change, MHAs and MPAs could still operate mixed together, although the alteration came particularly late in the day for the wagons as withdrawals were soon underway. These were still continuing in early 2023 with most months seeing 30 or so MHAs and MPAs consigned to scrap merchants as the introduction of the Wascosa-owned MLAs continued to make an impact.

ABOVE: Only an inspection of the wheel faces will reveal the difference between an MHA and MPA with 394107 displaying its revised code and painted out EWS lettering at Hinksey on April 12, 2022. The new code was applied in a variety of ways with either a completely new panel added or a partial alteration of the existing one, as here, usually with white letters. The large fence is the acoustic barrier built to screen the virtual quarry siding from nearby housing. Brian Daniels

LEFT: Running over 90 minutes late, 66095 passes Blagrove, on the outskirts of Swindon, with the 6M26 07.37 Westbury-Stud Farm ballast empties on May 14, 2014. Th leading half of the train is formed of two-axle boxes, the MTAs being easy to discern due to their lower height while the second and third wagons show the different look of a 16-rib and 11-rib MHA. At least one MFA is further back while nine JNA Falcons bring up the rear. Martin Loader

Modelling BR: Engineers Wagons of Privatisation 45

Railtrack renewal

ABOVE: Fitting plain disc braked wheels to the Accurascale MHA allows a MPA to be created, the left hand wheel face showing the difference compared to a stainless steel disc insert with bolt detail. The wagon has also been renumbered with Railtec custom panels.

Coalfish conversions

With both main types of MHA available ready-to-run in OO gauge, Terry Bendall sets out to bring a bit of variation to proceedings by modelling one of the MAA conversions as well as creating an MPA.

Modelling the MHA Coalfish in 4mm scale was made significantly easier towards the end of last year with Accurascale releasing RTR models of the 11-rib batch numbered 394500-999 and 396000-165, these appearing in EWS maroon, debranded maroon as used by DB and as the solitary DB red repaint 394829. These joined Hornby's much earlier model of the 16-rib wagons, 394001-400, which together cover the vast majority of requirements.

However, to add a bit of interest, it was also decided to model one of the five MAA conversions which were cut down to become 394406-410 as well as a recoded MPA with its different wheelsets. Starting with the latter, this is about as simple a conversion as possible as the wheelsets just need altering to have plain discs rather than a representation of the bolt-on discs.

Using one of the Accurascale MHA models as the basis, this had the supplied wheelsets with their very nice stainless steel disc inserts removed and replaced by the wheel assemblies out of one of the company's early period HAA hoppers. These had the disc brake friction surface cast into the wheel in the same manner as the MPAs, which is something recreated on the models, so a simple wheel swap gives the desired effect. Although the MPAs also had some minor brake rigging adjustments, this is not something that can be seen in model form.

Sleeper load

Other work on the MPA included removing the NEM coupling pockets, fitting Roxey screw couplings and adding homemade air pipes from brass wire. Seeking a different load to ballast for a change, it was decided to portray a wagon carrying recovered sleepers, which is something seen relatively often with these heading to one of Network Rail's track recycling centres.

The sleeper load was made using scale thickness and length plywood sleepers, which were coloured with wood stain and fitted with individual chairs from the C&L range, these receiving a coat of rust using Humbrol colours. Once finished, the sleepers and chairs were given a thin wash of Railmatch track colour to tone things down and then glued in place in the wagon. There is no neatness involved when loading recovered sleepers, these just being piled in on top of each other, so is easy to recreate, just ensuring that the sleepers are fully contained within the wagon and not piled too high.

With no MPA transfers yet available, a set of custom TOPS panels was ordered from Railtec, these being in white rather than yellow as was commonly used to recode the affected Coalfish. If using a wagon with the EWS lettering still in place, this should also typically be painted out. Finally, the last task was to weather the wagon, a variety of Humbrol browns being largely dry brushed on to tone down the factory colours. A similar approach can be taken for the inside before adding the load but using a mix of browns and greys.

Reusing a reject

When Hornby first released its Coalfish model almost 20 years ago, the results were, to be polite, not good, the resulting wagon

ABOVE: A load of recovered sleepers gives something a little different to ballast and is straightforward to make using plywood sleepers and separate chairs.

Railtrack renewal

ABOVE: **The original incarnation of the Hornby Coalfish was not a good model, but it can be repurposed as a cut-down ex MAA to a reasonable degree of authenticity by modifying the ends and capping.**

being chunky and dimensionally inaccurate. It was so poor that it was withdrawn soon after and completely re-tooled, this being the model that is available today.

However, the original body is a relatively good match for the five MHAs that were cut down from MAAs, these being slightly taller than the others. It will not give a perfect recreation as, for example, the body is a couple of millimetres too long but as a one-off to add a bit of interest to a rake, it is acceptable.

Some improvements are required though, most notably on the ends where five ribs were provided when it needs to be six. The three centre ones were therefore pared away with a scalpel and cleaned up with needle files with four replacements added using plastic strip. The body also lacks any representation of the chamfered lip around the top of the sides and ends. Plastic strip was again added all round and then profiled, this being trial and error to get something looking right as the moulded sides are overly thick so the additions have to be wider than they should to compensate.

If using a complete original model, then parts like the solebar steps and end grabs should also be replaced with items that are more to scale. In this case, it was just a body acquired second-hand that was being mounted on a spare HAA chassis, so this required all of the redundant hopper door and discharge fittings to also be carved away.

Adding the rust

Much of the remaining work focussed on the painting and weathering. When newly converted, the MAAs carried the Railfreight sub-sector colours, which employed Executive dark grey for the sides. However, as this faded and weathered, it took on a green tint, while the partial repaint carried out on cutting down the sides ensured that the top half of the wagon was in better condition than the bottom.

ABOVE: **Hornby's current Coalfish is a much more acceptable effort, representing the initial 400 wagons with 16 ribs converted in 1997/98. It sits well alongside the competition allowing the varied look of a rake to be reproduced.** Picture courtesy Kernow Model Rail Centre

The yellow ends were applied first, with some white added to fade the colour, while the inside was next sprayed with Railmatch light rust to serve as a base coat. When this was dry, the inside was masked and the bodysides sprayed with a mix of Humbrol 149 and 243, giving a green-tinged grey on which to weather. Railtec again provided a custom number panel for the model as this needed to fit in between two of the ribs, being just 5.5mm wide. While some of the wagons still had traces of their Railfreight Coal logos in place, this particular one did not so these were omitted. Once all the transfers were applied, these had a coat of matt varnish applied over the top.

The weathering employed a mix of dry brushing using various shades of Humbrol browns and washes of Railmatch sleeper grime applied over several days with time left for each application to dry before moving on to the next stage. Eventually, an acceptable representation of the finish compared to photos emerged with an overall coat of a thin wash of sleeper grime applied as the last step to tone everything down.

ABOVE: **With their original paintwork now over 30 years old, the ex MAAs that survive are not in good condition so plenty of rust is required. The number panel was again a custom job from Railtec due to the small space available.**

ABOVE: **The late series 11-rib MHA as supplied by Accurascale showing the three liveries currently available, EWS, DB red and debranded EWS.**

Modelling BR: Engineers Wagons of Privatisation 47

Railtrack renewal

MTA ballast wagons

Additional two-axle boxes for EWS were built on former TTA underframes and later joined by further conversions of the Limpets. Simon Bendall looks at their complex history while **Terry Bendall** upgrades the 4mm Bachmann model.

The MTA code first appeared in August 1998 when the 12 ZKA Doorands converted in 1993/94 were recoded and renumbered into their own series, becoming 395001-012. These had been part of the ZKA Limpet programme at the time but rather than just have the overloading slots cut into their sides, the dozen wagons had their bodysides and ends fully reduced in height to form low-sided ballast wagons. While they received a separate codename, they were confusingly numbered at random in the same series as the Limpets. All were finished in engineers' grey/yellow, and this was retained after becoming MTAs.

While these re-numberings were undertaken, a much more extensive conversion programme was getting underway as EWS had identified a need for further two-axle ballast and spoil opens to replace vacuum-braked wagons. Like the Limpets and Doorands, these were to be built on the reconditioned underframes of TTA tankers, the freight operator having secured over 200 examples from Shell, which were redundant following the withdrawal of the oil giant from using rail.

With RFS contracted to conduct the rebuilding, the first wagons were finished towards the end of 1998, but it was January 1999 before they began to roll out of Doncaster and into traffic, the number series beginning with 395013. By the end of the year, 200 examples had been completed with conversions ending with 395213, all carrying EWS maroon with yellow capping. The second half of 2000 then brought a further 28 rebuilds, adding 395214-241 to the total.

While the bodywork of 395013-241 was largely based on 395001-012, it was not identical. Most obvious was the ends, which were the same height as the sides on the batch of 228 while on the original dozen, they protruded several inches higher.

Limpets cut down

Further MTAs were created throughout 2007 as EWS reduced the bodywork height on the MKA/ZKA Limpets that remained in traffic, this taking place at Stoke and also Margam wagon repair depot. Renumbered into the 395251-405 series, the resultant wagons normally matched the appearance of 395001-012 with the ends being slightly taller than the sides. However, for no apparent reason, a small number of the wagons were cut down so that the ends were the same height as the sides, examples being 395296/301/373/377.

Fresh yellow paint was applied all round the top of the bodies, but the remainder of each wagon was not so lucky, retaining whatever livery was already carried. In most cases, this was dirt and rust with the underlying colour impossible to see but under the muck lurked various shades of grey, such as Yeoman, Transrail and Departmental, along with ARC mustard and Loadhaul black/orange. In some cases, what remained of the original ARC lettering and Yeoman 'Y' logo was also discernible.

Although the Coalfish name was originally applied to the MHAs, over time it came to encompass the MFA and MTA types as well from an operating point of view as they were essentially all a variation of the same design.

ABOVE: By March 2001, 395105 was some two years old when recorded at Didcot sandwiched in between an MHA and MFA 391102. Its appearance is entirely typical of the 395013-241 batch rebodied by RFS. Simon Bendall

ABOVE: Originally a ZKA Doorand converted in 1994, 395003 was one of the original 12 MTAs renumbered four years later. By September 12, 2006, its engineers' grey/yellow livery was all but obliterated under dirt and rust when recorded at Didcot. Brian Daniels

Railtrack renewal

However, experience of mixing the three types together resulted in the introduction of marshalling restrictions due to differences in the braking characteristics of the MHA/MPA compared to the MTA.

With two disc-braked wheels and two clasp brakes, the MHA/MPA had low brake force whereas the MTA, with four cast iron brake blocks, had high brake force. A rake of either was not a problem but mixing them, especially if poorly loaded, gave the potential for coupling snatches and derailments. As a result, an instruction was issued that no more than five of either type could be marshalled together in a mixed train, There was no restriction on the MFAs, so they were useful in helping to break up blocks of the other types.

The MTAs of all batches began to be removed from traffic around 2017 and declined substantially over the next two years. By 2020, just two of the 395001-012 batch remained in traffic while there were 20 of the ex-Limpets left and 100 of the EWS rebodies. Further reductions followed but a smattering of MTAs remained in traffic in the spring of 2023.

ABOVE: The MTA conversions that resulted from cutting down the MKA/ZKA Limpets in 2007 are illustrated by newly completed 395320 at Didcot on June 19 that year. The majority of these sported ends that were taller than the sides, setting them apart from the EWS rebodies. There was also some difference in the spacing of the bodyside ribs on some examples, depending on the origin of the donor wagon. Beneath some three decades of dirt, the wagon is still in ARC mustard with the lower section of the ARC lettering still visible. *Brian Daniels*

RIGHT: Although somewhat difficult to see, 395394 retains Loadhaul black and orange as it passes South Kenton in a Bescot-Wembley engineers on July 31, 2007, its freshly applied yellow band rather contrasting with the rest of the wagon. Other Loadhaul-liveried MTAs included 395296/328/339. *Timara Easter*

Re-springing the MTA

In common with the ZKA Limpets and Railtrack PNAs, the Bachmann OO gauge model of the MTAs uses the TTA chassis. As a result, it also has the incorrect style of spring fitted, featuring the original leaf design rather than the Bruninghaus replacements. It is a simple but worthwhile job to make the change by fitting the replacements available from S Kits or, an in this case, Stenson Models.

To do this, the existing mouldings were cut through close to the hangers and the W-irons using a pair of side cutters. The remainder of the spring moulding on each W-iron was then removed using a combination of a rotary cutting tool in a mini drill, a scalpel and a small screwdriver used as a chisel. Needle files were then used to smooth up the cut surfaces. The new spring castings were cleaned up and fixed in place using superglue and later painted once the glue had set. Other small jobs were fitting screw couplings from the Roxey Mouldings range and homemade air pipes formed from brass wire.

LEFT: The Bachmann MTA is seen with the replacement Bruninghaus spring castings in place. As the handbrake lever passes in front of one spring on each side, this needs to be temporarily prised off and then refitted after completion.

RIGHT: Once painted, the new springs will match the remainder of the chassis with any slight variation in finish masked by weathering once applied.

LEFT: Last year saw Bachmann release a new batch of its OO gauge MTAs, with models appearing in both Loadhaul and Civil Engineers colours as a representation of the cut-down Limpets. Both are numbered as examples that had their ends cut down to the same height as the bodysides so are accurate in this respect, but a few other compromises remain, such as the presence of solebar steps and bodyside grab rails. *Image courtesy Kernow Model Rail Centre*

Railtrack renewal

An array of flats

The first decade or so of privatisation saw a wide range of new flat wagon designs enter traffic, these either being new builds or conversions and largely belonging to Railtrack/Network Rail or EWS. **Simon Bendall** provides a round-up of the most important and modellable.

ABOVE: Displaced from refuse traffic, 34 FYA binliner flats were modified as FDA sleeper carriers in 2001 by EWS, receiving mesh decks, longitudinal timber baulks and ratchet strap tensioners. These were originally FGA outer Freightliner flats with drawgear at one end only so operated in pairs. Numbers were 621283, 621447/54/58/59/64/65/72/73/77/81/83/85-87/94/96/99, 621501/06/08/10/11/14/20/25/27/28/30-32/39/40/42. Pictured at Basford Hall on April 21, 2012, 621485 was in EWS maroon, which was applied during its binliner days. Initially used on construction of the Channel Tunnel Rail Link, withdrawal came around 2016 while conversion from the Bachmann FGA in 4mm would be relatively straightforward. Dan Adkins

LEFT: A more involved repurposing of displaced FYA binliner flats by EWS arrived in 2002 with 18 converted to single wagons by fitting drawgear at both ends. Each then received three 20ft modules featuring fixed ends and mesh drop-doors, these using the existing twistlocks to locate them. Reclassified as FJA Tench general materials carriers, they were renumbered as 621900-17 and helped replace the remaining BR-built YPA Tench. Retaining faded Railfreight red, 621905 passes Chesterfield South Junction on August 12, 2011, while running from Doncaster to Toton with a load of rails and crossing vees. Examples were still in traffic during 2022. Tim Rogers

Railtrack renewal

ABOVE: The Super Tench name was coined during 2010 for the repurposing of just six YQA Parr sleeper carriers by DB Schenker, these receiving very similar bodywork to the FJAs following the removal of their wooden floors. The modified wagons, DC967503/560/608/615/638/642, were neither recoded or renumbered, remaining mixed in with the remaining YLA Mullets and the now withdrawn Parrs, with some still in use in 2022. Revolution Trains is currently producing the Mullet, Parr and Super Tench family in both N and OO gauge with release scheduled for later this year. On August 12, 2011, DC967503 was bringing up the rear of the 6M73 10.52 Doncaster Decoy-Toton hauled by 66147 at Chesterfield, again with point components and rails as a load. Tim Rogers

RIGHT: During 2002, EWS converted two redundant YEA Perch long welded rail wagons into FZA for the conveyance of long switch and crossing assemblies, these being numbered 600501 and 600502 with the latter recorded at Didcot soon after completion. These joined the original 1983-built prototype Super Salmon DB996699, which was eventually similarly modified and renumbered as FZA 600500 in 2004. All three feature overhanging rails fixed to timber baulks on the deck with yellow-painted bolsters that can slide along the rails to support any length of point assembly loaded and lashed on top. Due to the long rails, the wagons always operate with a RRA under-runner at both ends. All three were still in traffic in 2023. Simon Bendall

LEFT: An early conversion by EWS in 1997 was to modify four RRA runner wagons into OSA sleeper carriers, 400170/230/284/287 receiving longitudinal timber baulks on their decks and ratchet tensioners along the sides. A strange modification due to their short length and limited capacity, the conversions were unsurprisingly not a great success and 400284 is seen back in use as an under-runner in Didcot Yard in 1999. This was accompanying the previously mentioned prototype DB996699, which was at this point classified as a YLA Mullet and yet to become an FZA. Simon Bendall

Modelling BR: Engineers Wagons of Privatisation 51

Railtrack renewal

ABOVE: Considerable investment was made in the fleet of continuously welded rail (CWR) trains early in the privatisation period by both Railtrack and then Network Rail. This initially involved refurbishing the existing fleets of YEA Perch and Porpoise with some wagons receiving Railtrack's green livery with silver lettering, as demonstrated by ex-works DB9797014 at Didcot Yard. *Simon Bendall*

LEFT: A number of former Cargowaggon IGA flats have been modified over the years to carry continuously welded rail, their principal domestic use being between Scunthorpe and Eastleigh while they also work through the Channel Tunnel from the continent with imported rail. Originally modified by GE Rail Services, the wagons now belong to Touax with the principal alteration being the red-painted frames to hold the rails. On April 15, 2016, 83 80 4736 144-2 passes Water Orton in the formation of the 6X01 Scunthorpe Trent Yard to Eastleigh East Yard. *Dan Adkins*

ABOVE: To expand and modernise the CWR trains or Rail Delivery Trains as they were increasingly known, Railtrack purchased a number of the former Tiphook KFA container flats owned by GE Rail Services in 2002. Some of these were extensively modified to feature new rail handling equipment on their decks. This included NLU93339, which was reclassified as a JZA, and is seen at Northampton on January 25, 2015, in the consist of a 6Y24 Harrow & Wealdstone to Basford Hall. Concurrently, WH Davis built two new wagon fleets to go with them and added an additional batch in 2005, NLU93600-17 being equipped with clamping banks to secure the rail in transit while NLU93700-73 feature roller racks to hold the rail. All were coded JZA as well with NLU93756 recorded at Hoo Junction on May 26, 2016. *Dan Adkins*

Railtrack renewal

ABOVE: Early 2001 saw the appearance of the first rail putler, this being an OBA open converted into an unloading chute for use with Perch or Salmons carrying continuously welded rail. The putler was positioned at one end of the rake with rail fed through the red-painted chutes at each end down onto the track. Little was left of the original OBA bodywork while a lightweight lifting gantry was installed at each of the putler to assist with deploying the chutes into position. Each conversion used equipment provided by Robel and was accompanied by a support van, which went at the other end of the train behind the loco when formed with the CWR wagons. At least three OBA wagons were converted, 110306/375/668, with 110306 recorded at Didcot in September 2002 with VAA 200162 in support. 110375 was the sole remaining example by 2012 but out of use. Simon Bendall

ABOVE: The 32 KRA sleeper carriers, JARV97101-32, were built at Doncaster in 1999-2000 for Jarvis, originally seeing use with its Fairmont Tamper P811-S track renewal machine DR78901. Following this machine's storage in 2006 and the collapse of the company, the wagons eventually passed into Network Rail ownership, being repainted from maroon to yellow and re-prefixed. On April 15, 2017, NR97105 passes Kingsthorpe in the consist of 6R02 Bescot-Bourne End Junction. Dan Adkins

ABOVE: Jarvis also invested heavily in creating Rail Delivery Trains (RDTs), which could offload continuously welded rail from one side using synchronised lifting gantries and then recover old rails onto the wagons to be removed for recycling. These were essentially a modernised version of the YFA Salmons used by BR with each set featuring five gantry-equipped YFA wagons and a sixth YXA vehicle carrying a generator to power the whole rake. Converted from Tiphook curtain-hood steel carriers, an initial three sets were introduced in 2001 with DR92503 and DR92516 recorded at Kingmoor Yard in June 2005. A number of additional trains were rapidly added so that by 2006, DR92571 was the highest number with the later conversions featuring more heavy-duty lifting and deck equipment along with larger generator sets. However, the collapse of Jarvis saw the trains stored and eventually scrapped. David Ratcliffe

Railtrack renewal

From the initial batch of 20 wagons, CAIB95623 was stabled in Tonbridge West Yard on September 7, 2004, with a bulldozer load, not long after the unloading ramp sections were retrospectively added. Pat Seale

KWA plant carriers

Once a key part of the engineers' fleet, the use of Lowmacs and other former BR special wagons ceased in the early years of privatisation. However, some attempt was made to replace them with a new fleet. **Simon Bendall** looks at their history while Terry Bendall tackles a 4mm scale kit.

By the mid-1990s, the remaining fleet of ex BR specially constructed wagons such as Lowmacs, Flatrols and Weltrols were already an operational headache. Not only were they elderly and speed-restricted, but they were also universally either vacuum-braked or unfitted. However, they still performed a number of useful roles, such as transporting the few remaining single line track relaying gantries. On the former Southern Region, a number of Lowmacs and Flatrols were also used by EWS to carry tracked heavy plant, such as bulldozers and excavators, to and from worksites across the region.

Initial proposals to repurpose car carriers and 'piggyback' wagons made little headway, leading to an eventual and perhaps somewhat reluctant order for modern replacements. Built by WH Davis, a fleet of 20 bogie well wagons were provided to Caib, which hired them to EWS for its Railtrack contract. These were numbered CAIB95610-29 and coded KWA with delivery to Hoo Junction taking place in the spring of 2001.

The wagons were rated to carry 18.6 tonnes and run at 60mph, with a stowage locker provided at one end. This held the straps used to secure the machines in place via

ABOVE: Also at Tonbridge as part of the same working on September 7, 2004, was CAIB95622 with an excavator on board. At a worksite, such a machine would use its jib to lift the square part of the ramp off the wagon and place it next to the well with the ramp then positioned next to it. The machine would then turn through 90 degrees and shuffle itself off. Pat Seale

Railtrack renewal

ABOVE: The grey livery carried by the second batch of Fastrols is demonstrated by VTG95632 at Eastleigh Yard on February 21, 2007, while carrying a rather non-standard sleeper load. Whether it had worked over the main line like this is unclear given the lack of load restraints. The fabricated Y25s used on the final ten wagons can be seen as can the twist-locks securing the ramp sections in place. As mentioned, the latter were retrofitted to the earlier wagons eventually. Brian Daniels

a combination of ratchet tensioners and lashing eyes. The livery was black with the sloping sections of the well finished in yellow as were the tensioners.

Second batch

With the KWAs proving to be a success and considerable improvement on the old wagons, they acquired the name Fastrols with a second order following in 2004. Again built by WH Davis, ten additional KWAs, VTG95630-39, were provided this time, albeit with some alterations, including the use of fabricated Y25 bogies instead of the cast Y25s employed under the initial wagons.

More noticeable was that each of the new batch had its own two-part ramp to help get the machinery on and off the wagon. In transit, the ramp sections sat atop the flat parts over the bogies, being held on by ISO-style twist-locks, while at a worksite, an excavator or similar would lift the ramps into place. The livery was also altered to VTG grey with the whole of the well area finished in yellow. By this time, bulldozers were the typical load as road/rail excavators had become more commonplace.

At the same time, the original 20 KWAs also received the two-part ramps but as these wagons were not fitted with the twist-locks, they were initially lashed on with straps. At some point later, they were further upgraded to feature the twist-locks and their associated supports on the deck. The wagons were also re-prefixed to VTG95610-29 to reflect the change of ownership but remained in their black livery.

Around 2010, the KWAs fell out of use as road/rail technology improved and protective boards were introduced so that bulldozers could use level crossings and transfer points to access the network without their tracks damaging the surfaces. Consequently, all of the KWAs have spent a number of years stored out of use at Hoo Junction and more recently Gascoigne Wood.

S Kits plant carrier

Back in 2007, S Kits released two versions of the KWA plant carriers in OO gauge, one covering the Caib batch with the other for the VTG wagons, each featuring the relevant style of bogies and other details as required. Pictured here is the Caib version, the construction being very easy as the entire wagon body is a one-piece resin casting. This is of a particularly high quality, featuring some very fine deck plating detail, and only requires the mould infeed to be removed from one end of the casting.

To the body were added the etched brass bufferbeams and plates for the TOPS number panels as well as the various shackles. The two-part ramps are whitemetal castings that go together without fuss as do the bogies, although on the model shown here, etched brass bogie centres were used rather than the provided whitemetal centres to allow easier conversion to P4 gauge. Finally, the remaining detail parts, such as the buffers and toolbox, can be added.

Painting was straightforward using Railmatch black and warning yellow. A suitable bulldozer load was sourced from the Norscot diecast construction machinery range which, although HO scale, looks the part once it has been toned down, while ratchet straps were added using slithers of Tamiya masking tape secured with varnish. The positioning of these was based on photos and an EWS loading diagram.

ABOVE: The Norscot bulldozer completes the KWA kit nicely, even if it is an HO scale model. However, with a distinct lack of modern plant available in 4mm scale, it is one of very few options.

ABOVE: The securing straps are made from slithers of Tamiya masking tape and can be secured in place with a dab of varnish if they come unstuck.

With no specific transfers available for the kit, the custom route was taken for the number panel as a first step. These were produced by Railtec using its bespoke TOPS panel ordering option where the required details and size were supplied and resulted in a set of waterslide transfers, including a spare, arriving not long after. Other small details came from Fox and Appleby sheets while options for the remainder will be explored later but a 2mm scale Caib logo may well be suitable for the opposite end.

Modelling BR: Engineers Wagons of Privatisation 55

Railtrack renewal

Salmons to Ospreys

The longest-lived of BR's purpose built engineers wagons, the Salmon and Osprey track panel carriers still remain a part of the modern infrastructure fleet, although not for much longer. **Gareth Bayer** details their history.

Still working hard for DB Cargo after more than six decades, the 62ft-long Salmon bogie rail wagons are incredible survivors. Based on a pre-nationalisation LMS design, some 500 examples made it through to 2000 and while this number has steadily declined, 15 years later there were still over 100 re-bogied YSA/YWA in traffic along with 200 YKA Osprey.

Built under 16 different lots to six diagrams, a number of famous names were involved in their construction. These included GR Turner of Langley Mill, Head Wrightson & Co of Thornaby-on-Tees, Teesside Bridge & Engineering in Middlesbrough, Powell Duffryn at Maindy Road, Cardiff, and the BR workshops at Derby and Wolverton. Differences between diagrams included bogie type (LMS 8ft, GWR 5ft 6in Plate or BR 8ft Plate) and the presence of side rails, bolsters, or both. The number series was DB996000-DB996677 and DB996804-DB997019.

Originally built without power brakes (TOPS code YMO) or with a through vacuum pipe (YMP), most of the Salmon fleet was given air brakes in the 1980s (YMA or YMB) with many gaining either all-over yellow or grey/yellow in the process. Other modifications included the removal of the side rails, bolsters, and end flaps along with the fleet-wide addition of corner steps and strap tensioner ratchets on the solebars. Around 90 vehicles were fitted with various types of extendable crane and later, in many cases, a protective roof for the loading and unloading of rails at possessions (YFA). Some also gained large wooden side and cross members for carrying concrete sleepers.

ABOVE: Built in 1958 by Teesside Bridge & Engineering to diagram 1/646, DB996530 featured BR 8ft Plate bogies and five bolsters for carrying rail. Fast forward 55 years and the YKA Osprey has ASF Ride Control bogies and new body hardware for the secure location of track panels. It is pictured at Didcot on March 6, 2012, still carrying its Salmon name on the solebar. *Gareth Bayer*

RIGHT: Showing how the Ospreys look when empty, DB996483 was the leading wagon of an engineers' service at Water Orton on March 22, 2012 with 66167 in charge. Visible in the chain box on the underframe are ratchet straps while the angled section of the trussing just about retains yellow EWS lettering on a red background. *Mark Franklin*

Railtrack renewal

ABOVE: Four detail views of the principal modifications made to the YKA Ospreys, showing the end pillars and centre stanchions. The bufferbeams also received a new coat of yellow paint during the conversion, this sometimes extending up onto the floor. *Mick Bryan*

American bogies

The original diagram 1/640 wagons with LMS 8ft bogies had almost disappeared by privatisation, but the rest of the fleet was still important for transporting sleepers and track panels. However, their operation was hampered by the 5ft 6in and 8ft Plate bogies, which were restricted to 40mph or 50mph and required frequent maintenance of their troublesome plain bearing axleboxes.

With the Salmons having clocked up over four and a half decades of service, EWS commenced an upgrade programme in 1998, which eventually saw over half of the remaining fleet of YMA wagons re-bogied. These received an American-manufactured three-piece Ride Control bogie with roller bearings from ASF. A small number of YFAs were also provided with new bogies, losing their cranes and roofs (if still fitted) at the same time.

The first 124 Salmons fitted with the new bogies were given the TOPS code of YSA but were still rated at 50mph, albeit with significantly improved reliability. A second group of vehicles, outshopped from the following year, were recoded YWA with a 60mph maximum speed. In conjunction with the bogie swap, the obsolete end footsteps were removed on the majority of vehicles and a brake handwheel fitted to all four corners of the wagon, operating the closest bogie only.

Some wagons, mostly former YFA, with steps in non-standard positions retained them, while the new handwheels, which were of the four spoke 'press stud' style, usually did not match what was already fitted! Eventually, 317 Salmons were cycled through the re-bogieing programme between 1998 and 2008, creating a fleet of 124 YSAs and 193 YWAs. The remaining unconverted YMAs with their Plate bogies were stored in 2006. During 2008/09, there was a further upgrade for the YSA Salmons to give them the same 60mph maximum speed as the later conversions, bringing re-coding as YWA.

Taking flight

A number of incidents involving improperly secured track panels becoming out of gauge during transit led to a new modification programme which began in May 2009. The wagons were fitted with two large rectangular pillars with a triangular support at each end spaced to accept a standard 60ft track panel, along with two slightly off-centre stanchions. The pillars are wide enough to fit within the track gauge, locking the track in place, and tall enough to secure three panels. The new hardware does not completely avoid the need for strapping in every case and it is still common to see panels that are shorter than 60ft secured to the wagons in this way.

The first 21 conversions (DB996102, 996323/42/48/50/60, 996402/11/51/90/99, 996508/79, 996612/49/51, 996867, 996915/32/54 and DB997006) involved YSA wagons and were undertaken at Axiom Rail's Stoke-on-Trent works and the former Crewe Diesel Depot. Initially recoded YWA reflecting their concurrent uprating to 60mph, they were quickly recoded YKA. They also received the new name Osprey, which was not physically carried on the wagons. The use of the name osprey, a traditional predator of salmon and other fish, would appear to have been an inside joke courtesy of the DB staff responsible for the modifications. The first batch of Osprey was formed of 50 vehicles but eventually 200 were quickly completed by the end of November 2009.

The Ospreys were deployed in the same way as the Salmons and other track panel carriers. They can be seen in small numbers in a train with any other infrastructure vehicles, such as autoballaster hoppers or two-axle and bogie spoil carriers or used in longer formations. They can carry up to three 60ft panels, either recovered track with wooden sleepers or brand new concrete-sleepered sections.

In subsequent years, some Ospreys have lost their stanchions and reverted back to Salmons but much of the fleet has remained in use along with the YWA Salmons. Only now in 2023 are the two fleets facing replacement with the arrival of the Wascosa-owned FEA flats and their track-carrying modules. However, with these still being introduced and modified, mass replacement was still pending by the spring.

RIGHT: **DB996241 is one of the small number of Ospreys to have retained footsteps by virtue of them being located in non-standard positions, something that was especially common on the former YFA crane-fitted Salmons. Pictured at Crewe on March 14, 2010, the wagon is carrying a partial load of concrete sleeper track panels, this just being long enough to lock around the stanchions so not requiring ratchet straps.** *Mark Franklin*

Modelling BR: Engineers Wagons of Privatisation **57**

Railtrack renewal

ABOVE: **The typical look of a loaded Osprey is captured by DB993634 with the cast ASF bogies shown to advantage.**

Modelling flying fish

Having covered the prototype history, Mick Bryan describes how to convert the 4mm scale Cambrian YSA/YWA Salmon kit into the modified YKA Osprey track carriers.

One of the regular freight trains passing my back door since late 2008 has been the 6K05 Carlisle Yard-Crewe Basford Hall infrastructure service, this being a suitable candidate to model for use on both my own and my local club's layouts. Fortunately, I could often photograph 6K05 during breaks from work, with one of the common wagon types observed being Salmons of the YSA and YWA variety. Now one of the oldest designs on the network, the Salmons in their various forms are still going today and make for an attractive model.

At the time, Cambrian Models was about to release its long-lived Salmon plastic kit in updated form with modern ASF bogies, so the YSA and YWA variants were on the cards to be modelled. Then the YKA Osprey conversions started to appear in traffic. Fitted with substantial metal stanchions, these modified wagons were designed to carry 60ft track panels without the need to secure the load in place with ratchet straps. This removed the need for staff to climb over the wagons with the associated health and safety paranoia and also reduced the risk of the track panels shifting out of gauge during transit due to being poorly secured.

Several weeks later, a few YKAs turned up on 6K05 and my decision to model them was made. I was lucky enough to obtain drawings of the new stanchions while, soon afterwards, my local line was being re-laid and a train of 22 YKAs awaiting loading with track panels appeared outside my back door. Needless to say, the opportunity was not wasted, and I photographed as many as I could!

Now that I had the donor wagons sorted and a collection of photographs, consideration was next given to the construction of the stanchions. Should I make them from brass or plastic? Do I make them as unloaded or loaded and if the latter, how do I go about modelling suitable track panels and should they be built to OO, EM or P4 gauge? Following discussions on the forum of Diesel & Electric Modellers United (DEMU), I decided to go for the P4 option as the width of the stanchions would look narrow if loaded with OO gauge track, even though the wagons were to run on a OO layout.

ABOVE: **Many livery variations can be found across the Ospreys, DB996512 having unusual, yellow-painted trussing.**

ABOVE: **Due to the height of the stanchions, Ospreys are limited to carrying three 60ft track panels, this being somewhat different to their Salmon days when the stack could be double this.**

Railtrack renewal

With five Cambrian Salmons initially purchased with the intention of making four YKAs and one YWA, as the project progressed, I decided to make all of them as YKAs. I had planned on using Romford 10.5mm disc wheels but then discovered the Kadee 520 10.5mm disc wheels then stocked by DC Kits. Not only were these of excellent quality but they were also considerably cheaper than the Romford option so, with the saving I made for five wagons, I bought another Salmon kit!

Building and converting

The Cambrian kits were built as per the instructions with the exception of the buffers and handbrake wheels. The Ospreys that I had photographed carried three types of buffers, from the original short-stepped type to Dowty and Blair oval varieties. The kit buffers were lacking in detail, so I replaced them with cast whitemetal versions from MJT (reference no. 2352 Oleo oval) and Appleby Model Engineering (original Salmon and Blair) on two wagons each.

For reasons unknown, most of the Ospreys that I had seen had four or six-spoke brake handwheels at one end and a four-spoke cut-out version at the other. These were sourced from the excellent Stenson Models range and mounted on 1 x 1.5mm strips of plastic. One other modification I carried out was to reinforce the underframe trussing with round plastic rod glued inside the angle, as past experience of these wagons showed that this is a vulnerable area unless very carefully handled. I only reinforced the outer trusses as these are the ones that suffer the most.

Although the drawings provided were helpful, they did not show the actual dimensions of the stanchions, so I had to 'guesstimate' using my photographs and comparing them to the depth and width of the track panel load. By now, I had also decided that I would make the stanchions from plastic strip as this would be easier to work with and, due to their relatively small size, would not prove too fragile for handling at exhibitions.

The end stanchions were mainly constructed from Plastruct 3.2mm channel section (reference no. 90533). The prototype stanchions themselves are mounted on a thick piece of steel plate, which is bolted to the chassis. The plate was represented by 3mm x 30mm five thou plasticard and I made the first test stanchion on the bench. Unfortunately, the solvent caused the thin sheet to curl around the vertical sections, so the production stanchions were made in-situ on the wagons, with the mounting strip already fixed to the wagon so that it remained flat.

The vertical sections are 12mm high and 12mm apart on the inner edges. The 19mm long diagonal stiffener was made by filing back the channel section flanges at the ends and sliding it in between the uprights. The upper cross section was a 15mm piece of channel with the long edges rounded off with a file and the outer edges chamfered and fitted with five thou plasticard to represent the bevelled ends. The ends were completed with a strip of 1mm square Plastruct (no. 90740) at the outer edge.

The central stanchion supports were made using 14mm long and 2.5mm square Plastruct (no. 90770) for the uprights and 24mm long sections for the lower crosspiece. The crosspiece was filed down to about 2mm square as it is smaller in size than the uprights. Small fillets of five thou plastic strips were fitted for the strengthening plates on the lower angled joint and also for the small triangular guides on the top of the posts. These centre stanchions were also made in-situ on mounting plates already fixed to the wagon floor. These stanchions are not actually mounted dead centre, instead they are offset from the centre of the wagon by 6mm to the left, when viewed from the side with the chain box, to allow for the sleeper spacing of the track panels.

Finishing off

The Cambrian ASF bogies are a one-piece moulding and are very easy to assemble with brass bearings and outer cosmetic bearing covers fixed on afterwards.

ABOVE: **The idea of the Osprey conversions was to retain track panels without the need to lash them down. Partial panels can be carried in this manner if they are long enough to reach the central posts, otherwise they must be tied down conventionally.**

ABOVE: **If the track panels are made a snug fit on the model, they can be simply lifted off to allow the wagons to run empty. The ratchet straps stuffed into the underframe chain box are a common feature of the type.**

Modelling BR: Engineers Wagons of Privatisation **59**

Railtrack renewal

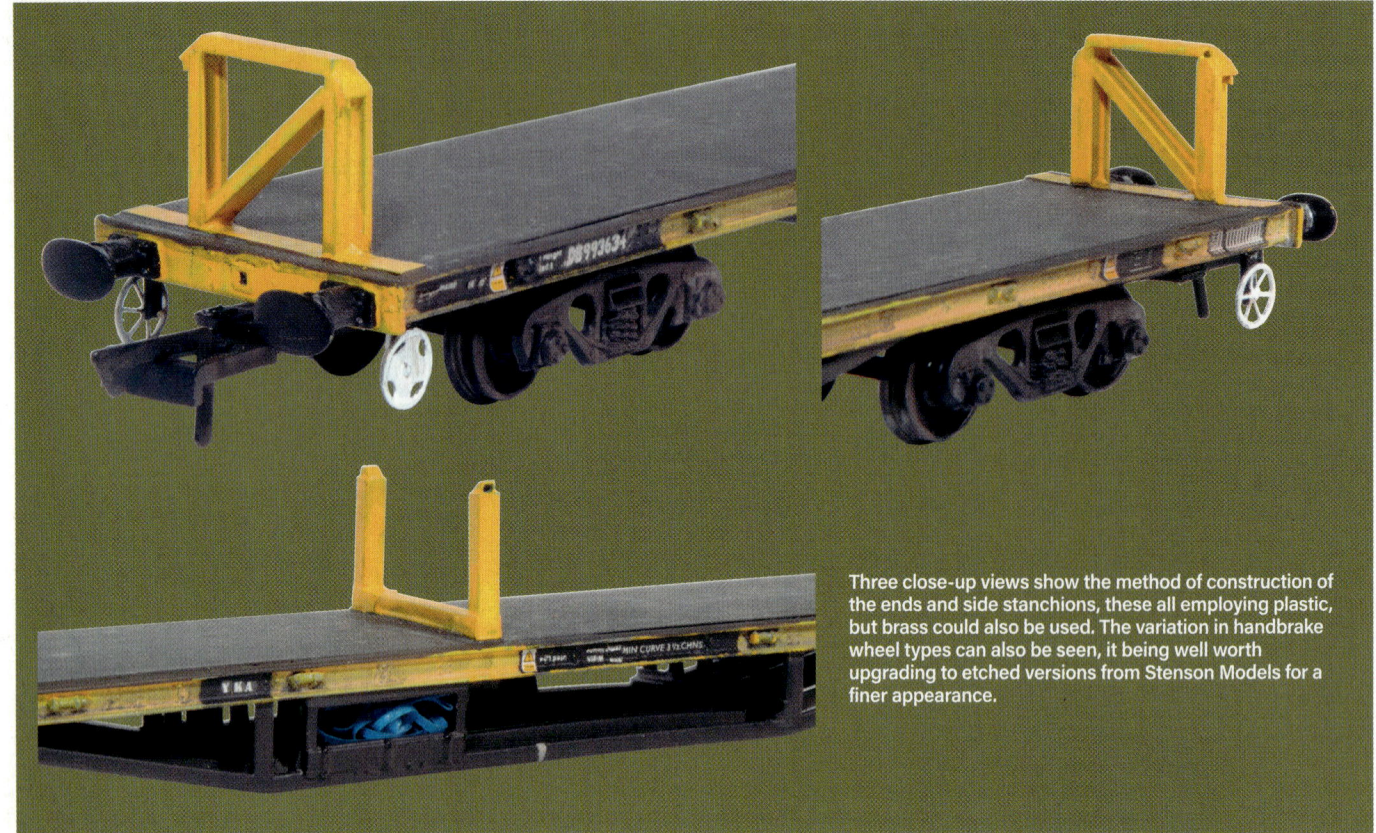

Three close-up views show the method of construction of the ends and side stanchions, these all employing plastic, but brass could also be used. The variation in handbrake wheel types can also be seen, it being well worth upgrading to etched versions from Stenson Models for a finer appearance.

I had a minor problem with the bogie pivot moulding as the original one supplied with the kit (with a square arrangement of mounting pegs to fit the square moulded underneath the floor) is not a snug fit in the coned hole of the one-piece bogie. There are pivots supplied with the new bogies that fit well within the coned hole, but the base is rectangular rather than square! This was cured by placing the rectangular base as centrally as possible on the edges of the square moulding on the underside of the floor. I did check that the buffer height was not compromised as this would effectively make the wagons ride higher on the bogies.

There is no definitive paint scheme for the Ospreys. The only common factor is the bright yellow of the stanchions, which contrasts with the grime, rust and whatever paint is still retained on the wagons. Most YKAs are painted yellow but there is great variety in the size and quantity of the black patches under the numbers and other painted data. Some still carry engineers' olive green under the grunge, but these appear more black than anything else after so many years.

In many cases, I had to confirm the numbers by looking at the builder's plate such is the poor state of the lettering. Within the 22 that I photographed, I found one with Mainline Freight brandings on the underframe trussing along with TLF South East and EWS on others. Transfers are from a mixture of Cambrian, Modelmaster and Fox. None of those that I photographed carried the Osprey codename with some still retaining the Salmon branding. A couple of variations exist in the yellow at the ends depending upon whether the section of the floor between the bufferbeam and the stanchion has been repainted or not. Weathering was carried out using an airbrush and dry brushing methods.

Loading up

After looking at various makes of track, I opted for the P4 gauge components then produced by Exactoscale. These had a decent thickness of sleeper when compared to other manufacturers. I used the 4FT101A bases and 4RA101B bullhead rail, cut into 240mm lengths to represent 60ft track panels. As these were going to be very visible and not covered in ballast, I had to remove all of the webbing between the sleepers with a nice sharp pair of flush-cut side cutters. This amounted to 1,600 or so cuts for the loads for six wagons!

A number of the sleepers moved along the rail during this process, but I created a template by spraying a section of track with webbing still in place with track colour. This image was then used to realign the cut sleepers before also spraying these with track colour and sleeper grime, using the paint to prevent the sleepers sliding along the rail. Rust coloured paint was then run along the railheads to simulate recently lifted track. One of the wagons carries a part load and this has to be strapped down conventionally. I have used 1mm wide masking tape for the ratchet straps. For this purpose, the wagons usually carry a couple of straps in the chain box under the solebar and I have represented these with strips of 1mm masking tape 'stuffed' into the box.

The track panels add a bit of weight, but the wagons have also been additionally ballasted should I wish to run them empty. I used liquid lead underneath the floor, held in place using Klear floor polish. The original intention was to use thin PVA glue to secure the liquid lead but after reading of potential expansion problems, I opted to use this alternative method. Although Klear is no longer readily available, any other varnish could easily be used.

As with other projects, I have found the DEMU forum a helpful place to bounce ideas around, particularly with regard to the track panel loads for these wagons. If you are not already a member of the Diesel & Electric Modellers United society (www.demu.org.uk), which then gives access to the forum, then I can thoroughly recommend it.

LEFT: With the bright yellow posts, the Ospreys certainly stand out as something a little different. With both Footplate Models and soon Hornby offering RTR Salmons in 4mm scale, it will be interesting to see if either develops a model of the Ospreys.

MAIL ORDER

RAILWAYS OF ASIA: SOUTH KOREA AND TAIWAN — NEW

World Railways Series, Vol 8
With over 180 colour photographs, this book offers a visual record of travels around South Korea and Taiwan, incorporating important historical events and technological developments and enticing visitors from around the world.

ONLY £16.99

Paperback, 96 Pages
Code: **KB0293**

Subscribers call for your £2 discount

ELECTROSTAR: CAPITAL COMMUTER — NEW

Britain's Railways Series, Vol 48
This book gives an overview of the routes they have worked, or are still working, as well as the different companies that these unsung heroes of the everyday railway have served.

ONLY £15.99

Paperback, 96 Pages
Code: **KB0306**

Subscribers call for your £2 discount

IRISH RAILWAYS: 100 YEARS

World Railways Series, Vol. 7
With over 190 pictures, both classic and modern, this volume explores the past, present and future of Ireland's evocative railways.

ONLY £16.99

Paperback, 96 Pages
Code: **KB0200**

Subscribers call for your £2 discount

CLASS 47s: JACK OF TRADES

Britain's Railways Series, Vol. 45
With over 230 images, this book showcases the versatility of the Class 47 and how it truly is the jack of all trades.

ONLY £16.99

Paperback, 96 Pages
Code: **KB0196**

Subscribers call for your £2 discount

THE MODERN RAILWAY

The 2023 edition of this sought-after 208 page hardback book comprises a directory of almost 3,000 rail businesses and suppliers with comprehensive contact information details.

ONLY £25.00

Paperback, 208 Pages
Code: **KB0233**

Subscribers call for your £2 discount

CLASS 73s

Britain's Railway Series, Vol 41
As the 73/9s continue to find work around the UK, it seems they may be part of the railway scene for a long while to come. With over 220 images, this book shows off all the sub-classes of the 73s and their work around the country.

ONLY £15.99

Paperback, 96 Pages
Code: **KB0262**

Subscribers call for your £2 discount

---

shop.keypublishing.com/books
Or call **UK: 01780 480404** - **Overseas: +44 1780 480404**

Monday to Friday 9am-5:30pm GMT. Free 2nd class P&P on all UK & BFPO orders. Overseas charges apply. All publication dates subject to change

TO VIEW OUR FULL RANGE OF BOOKS, VISIT OUR SHOP

High capacity upgrades

The traditional look of ballast trains under BR had been of low-capacity two-axle wagons trundling about at low speeds. This changed under Railtrack and Network Rail with numerous orders for large bogie wagons that had the capabilities to match aggregates designs. Simon Bendall **looks at the developments.**

The aggregates industry had recognised the benefits of employing large capacity wagons to transport its products in the late 1970s with the introduction of the first bogie hopper designs. This process only accelerated during the next decade with new or redeployed box wagons joining an assortment of colourful hoppers as companies sought to move away from the ageing and low-capacity fleets provided by BR.

The same development came to the power station coal industry from 1994 as National Power unveiled its new hopper wagon fleets to revolutionise the transport of coal and limestone to Drax. However, what these upgrades all had in common was the use of private finance to fund the rolling stock available.

With BR under-funded as a whole in the early 1990s, and the engineers' fleet even more so, there was little hope of seeing such high capacity stock introduced in large numbers for lowly infrastructure work. A glimmer of what was possible arrived early in 1993 with Network SouthEast unveiling its Skako auto-ballasting train, the ten YDA Octopus hoppers featuring remote-controlled discharge chutes for precision laying. Even today in 2023, the set remains in use with DB Cargo, albeit somewhat sporadically, around Central Scotland and northern England.

Going large

The Skako was an exception though and there was certainly no money to completely replace the array of two-axle ballast opens, where low-capacity rebuilds, such as the Sea Urchins, were the best options to make use of what conversion fodder was available. Even in the earliest years of privatisation, the practice of putting new bodies on old chassis with the Coalfish continued despite the limitations.

It took the unplanned repurposing of a third of the MBA 'monster box' fleet to bring US-style 'gondola' wagons to the British network for ballast and spoil work in 2000. The resulting low-sided MCA and MDA wagons showed the benefits of such stock for infrastructure purposes and all subsequent orders for ballast wagons intended for possession work over the past two decades have followed the same design template.

Meanwhile, the Skako showed that high capacity hoppers with automatic discharge were the way forward, both reducing the amount of labour required and allowing for faster and more efficient ballasting of newly laid track. The occasional hire of the Redland, later Lafarge, self-discharge trains were also beneficial in speeding the creation of track-beds, allowing a large quantity of ballast to be discharged for spreading in a relatively short time.

This experience helped shape requirements when it came to Railtrack placing significant orders for new wagons in 2001, although it was successor Network Rail that largely reaped the benefits. The fact that the autoballasters are still used intensively after two decades is a testament to their design. The high output ballast cleaner (HOBC) sets built by Plasser & Theurer have also proved to be a success, the mammoth trains being periodically upgraded and replaced with older sets sold abroad for further use.

The MRA side-tippers, with their re-working of the Mermaid concept, have proven to be the least successful aspect of the early 2000s acquisition spree, going on to be considerably under-utilised, certainly as intended. With more than half of the fleet now in the throes of rebuilding, Network Rail has come full circle and is once again re-purposing old stock!

> **BELOW:** The high output ballast cleaner sets blur the lines between on-track plant and wagons, their numbering and method of operation certainly putting them in the former category. For this special, the focus is on what could be considered traditional wagons, which are both easier to model and much more readily available In model form. While there are HO scale kits of HOBC wagons, these are European versions that differ somewhat from the YDA Octopus used in the UK. On April 12, 2021, 57002 passes Kintbury, west of Newbury, with the 6Z86 08.55 Taunton Fairwater-West Ealing taking a number of YDA for maintenance at the Plasser workshops. Martin Loader

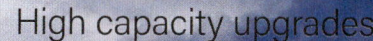
High capacity upgrades

MRA side-tippers

There was some surprise when Network Rail ordered a new fleet of side-tipping ballast wagons at the beginning of this century, such wagons having not been constructed since the final BR Mermaids 40 years earlier. The MRAs have since seen a mixed career with many now being rebuilt into conventional ballast boxes as **Simon Bendall** details.

The prototype for what would become the MRAs appeared in September 2000 with Thrall Europa rolling out JQA TCMC28200 from York Works. Based on the bogie box side tippers built by Standard Wagon in the mid-1980s, the wagon was rated for 75mph. Finished in a similar dark green colour to the Railtrack PNA/JNA fleets, the demonstrator was branded 'Thrall Europa'. The wagon subsequently underwent a series of running trials along with load tests, the latter evaluating the effectiveness of the two side-tipping boxes mounted on the vehicle's substantial underframe.

The demonstrator was sufficiently successful to persuade Railtrack to order what would become a fleet of 300 MRA wagons in early 2001 as part of a £40m investment in its infrastructure fleet, this also including the autoballasters. The first completed wagon, 501061, appeared that April for acceptance testing at Derby carrying Railtrack-branded beige with a blue stripe.

This wagon was initially uniquely coded as an MRA(D) on the TOPS computer system as it featured buffers and a screw coupling at both ends to allow for testing, but later was altered into an MRA(B) outer with conventional drawgear at one end only and a bar coupling at the other. Physically, the wagon was always lettered as an MRA(B) while, like the rest of the fleet, it was rated for 60mph with a gross laden weight of 90 tonnes.

Production batch

Deliveries of the production build of MRAs commenced soon afterwards and had been completed by mid-2002, the 300 wagons being formed up as 60 semi-permanently coupled five-wagon sets. Each set consisted of an outer with a generator, which were MRA(A) 501001-060, a non-generator outer numbered MRA(B) 501061-120 and three inners, which became 501121-300 as MRA(C).

During 2003, the entire fleet received an extension on the lower discharge doors, this being in the form of a distinctive ribbed section above the blue band. As these new parts obscured the wagon repeater numbers along the top of the bodies, these had to be applied on the extensions as well. Following the demise of Railtrack, the MRAs were eventually rebranded with Network Rail logos applied over the top of the Railtrack lettering.

ABOVE: **The prototype Thrall Europa-built JQA side-tipper TCMC28200 stands in York Works on March 3, 2001. Although unveiled the previous autumn, tipping trials were still being conducted at this point including the use of both ballast and coal as loads. Once deliveries of the Railtrack order commenced, the prototype faded from view.** Mark Saunders

BELOW: **Brand new MRA(C) inner 501279 was engaged on one of its first relaying jobs at Markshall Farm, near Norwich, on February 24, 2002. This shows the original look of the lower discharge door without the ribbed extension above the blue band and with the upper bodyside repeater numbers not obscured.** Tim Horn

Modelling BR: Engineers Wagons of Privatisation

High capacity upgrades

LEFT: Generator wagon 501024 shows off the next stage in the development of the MRAs at Derby in February 2004. This has received the ribbed extension on the lower doors, these covering the original upper body repeater numbers, which can just be seen behind the flap. As a result, new ones had to be added in front. As the generator took up extra space and contributed additional weight, both ballast boxes were smaller on the MRA(A) to compensate, compared to the rest of the set. *Simon Bendall*

RIGHT: With Network Rail logos now covering the Railtrack lettering, MRA(C) 501159 reposes in the autumn sunshine at Derby Litchurch Lane on October 13, 2010. This has remained the look of the initial 300 wagons ever since, just with increasing amounts of dirt and rust. *Simon Bendall*

In operation, the MRAs were used to lay foundation ballast, whereby a rake would be positioned on an adjacent line and each box tipped one at a time using remote control. The ballast would then by spread by bulldozers and similar to form the bed on which track panels would be laid. The hydraulics were arranged to allow the boxes to be tipped in either direction, avoiding the need for the wagons to arrive at a worksite a particular way round.

Mellow yellow
A further batch of 100 MRAs were constructed by Thrall's successor Trinity Rail at its Astra Vagoane plant in Romania during 2004. These wagons were to a Mk.2 design and featured a revised style of plain lower discharge doors, while the livery was now Network Rail yellow.

Formed in five-wagon sets with buffers and a screw coupling at the outer ends only again, the numbering was as follows: outers with generator 501301-320 MRA(D), outers 501321-340 MRA(E) and inners 501341-400 MRA(F).

During 2006, 25 MRAs were transferred to GB Railfreight for use on the Metronet contract in exchange for 50 MLAs going the opposite way. However, rather than receive the lemony yellow shade used on the other Metronet stock, 501301-05/21-25/41-55 simply gained new Metronet, GBRf, and London Underground logos on the existing livery in place of the Network Rail branding. These remain in use with GBRf today but typically with some or all of the logos removed or painted over, either deliberately in some cases or thanks to graffiti removal.

In a handful of cases, generator wagons have been repaired using a generator taken from a wagon in a different livery, for example 501036/52/54 all have a yellow casing while 501313 is the opposite with a beige generator standing out on the otherwise yellow wagon.

Tippers no more
As mentioned in the virtual quarry section, a number of MRA sets have suffered from generator failure and other mechanical issues over the years, leaving them unable to operate as intended. As the fleet has never been the most intensively used, repairs were not conducted with some affected sets instead relegated to bulk ballast flows to and from virtual quarries, these being loaded and unloaded conventionally using grabs. By the start of 2016, these were receiving additional lettering stating, 'Bulk ballast use only' and 'Generator disabled'.

Due to the under-use, the autumn of 2021 saw Network Rail announce that at least 250 of the MRAs are to be rebuilt as new bulk ballast wagons coded JNA-Y. The conversions, which are ongoing at Loram's workshops in Derby, involve reusing the chassis and fitting a new heavily ribbed box body on top. The fixed formation sets have also been abandoned with all wagons receiving buffers and a screw coupling at both ends.

Initially, the project got off to a slow start while design and acceptance work was conducted, but the first completed wagon emerged in June 2022, this being numbered 81 70 5831 001-8 and finished in Network Rail yellow. By the following spring, almost 100 wagons had been completed with examples despatched to York, Toton and Bescot among other locations from where they were beginning to enter traffic.

ABOVE: From the Romanian-built Mk.2 batch, MRA(E) outer 501331 displays its Network Rail livery at Kingsthorpe, Northampton, on December 4, 2016. These incorporated the lower door extension from new, allowing it to be plain steel sheet, the difference being obvious when compared to adjacent 501106. The wagon was forming part of a 6R06 North Wembley Junction-Basford Hall return empties. *Dan Adkins*

High capacity upgrades

LEFT: Although built for Network Rail, MRA(F) 501352 was one of the 25 wagons exchanged with GBRf two years after construction and rebranded for use on the Metronet contract. By December 13, 2014, some of this revised branding had also gone when the inner was recorded at Tonbridge West Yard. The 'AR' and 'BR' codes referred to box A and B, right hand side and assisted the operator using the remote control equipment.
Simon Bendall

ABOVE: With its generator disabled, MRA(A) 501027 was in bulk ballast traffic when recorded at Hellifield on August 9, 2018. The white on black lettering denoting this demotion had appeared on the doors and generator of such sets a couple of years earlier and led to the decision to rebuild over half of the fleet with new bodywork. Railtec offers transfers for the additions in 4mm scale. David Ratcliffe

Dapol MRA models

To date, only Dapol has tackled the MRAs in model form, releasing RTR models of both batches in OO gauge a decade ago. Curiously, no sooner had they appeared after a long gestation than they disappeared again with no subsequent re-runs. As a result, second-hand prices are now considerable with the models having been supplied in five-wagon boxsets complete with prototypical bar couplings between wagons and tension locks at the outer ends only.

Although a little basic in places, the models have plenty of potential with a bit of detailing and enhancing along with some much needed weathering, particularly to tone down the yellow versions. Dapol opted to build some 'play value' into the MRAs by making the ballast boxes poseable in a tipped position and the lower doors able to be partially opened for static use. As a result, none of the boxes are fixed to the chassis, merely locating on top, so securing these in place would be a first job for many.

A compromise has been made with the Axle Motion bogies as the plastic handbrake wheels are mounted on diagonally opposite sideframes on the model rather than both sides of one bogie. This allows the same bogie moulding to be used throughout and is a relatively easy fix.

Another area for attention is the sides of the metal weights that form the base of the ballast boxes beneath the doors. Sprayed to match the plastic, the colour density is variable on the yellow MRAs with some boxes being fine and others less so. The burr marks on the sides of the weights are also visible beneath the paint in some places. Fortunately, this area is prone to collecting dirt so is relatively easy to obscure under a coat of weathering.

Both of the sets pictured also have a variety of printing errors and omissions, the repeater numbers behind the door flaps are missing for example. There are also items in the wrong positions and even a repeated spelling mistake so something of a curate's egg. Nonetheless, the basis is there for a nice model and the etched details included around the generator are excellent.

ABOVE: The generator wagon from the Network Rail yellow release, although the TOPS code is incorrect, being labelled as an MRA(F) when it should be a (D).

ABOVE: The Network Rail beige/blue version is the better finished of the two pictured here, although some of the lettering positions are awry.

LEFT: One of the ballast boxes in the posed tipped position, the black clips being inserted to hold the body in place. On the far side, the door flap can also be seen lowered.

Modelling BR: Engineers Wagons of Privatisation **65**

High capacity upgrades

The Autoballasters

The Network Rail JJA and HQA autoballaster wagons have formed the backbone of the track renewals fleet for over two decades, working to every corner of the country. **David Ratcliffe** recounts their development and subsequent use.

During 1995, with a view to finding a replacement for the aging and labour-intensive BR-built Seacow and Sealion ballast hoppers, Transrail commissioned the conversion of one of the Tiphook Rail-owned 90-tonne GLW KPA bogie aggregate hoppers. Built by Arbel-Fauvet, 83 70 6905 048-7 was modified at RFS, Doncaster, into the first of the autoballasters.

This was fitted with four new hydraulically operated and remotely controlled discharge doors on each side between the bogies, subsequently going on trial at various engineers' yards around the country. The following year saw a further nine Tiphook KPA hoppers modified in the same way at Doncaster, 83 70 6905 104/10/13/24/28/51/70/73/75 joining the prototype in forming a ten wagon autoballaster set. In addition to being fitted with the new doors, which were supplied by the American company Difco, the end ladders were removed, and a canopy added above the end platform.

Initially, an air supply to operate the doors was provided by the attached loco but as trials progressed, this was found to be variable depending on what class was attached. With the installation of solebar lighting also a desirable upgrade, 1998 saw a redundant Tiphook KOA 'piggyback' wagon assigned to accompany the set. This carried a mobile generator to power the lights as well as a compressor for the air supply, air tanks additionally being fitted on top to create a reservoir. The same year saw the train hired to track maintenance company GTRM, working out of the virtual quarry at Guide Bridge with the hoppers' dark blue livery gaining the company's logos.

Production conversions

Evidently they were a success as a further ten autoballaster conversions were ordered by GTRM, these incorporating a number of upgrades. The most notable was that one wagon per five-vehicle set featured a large onboard generator, this being mounted at one end beneath a protective cover. One generator could power ten wagons across two sets with the other acting as a back-up in case of failure during a possession.

When delivered at the end of 2000, the ten wagons were renumbered and re-coded, becoming JJAs GERS12901-10 and all finished in a cream livery with maroon pinstripes and GTRM logos. The livery was altered after 2002 following the merger of GTRM, Centrac and Carillion to create one large track maintenance company under the Carillion brand. As well as new logos, the colour of the stripes was changed from maroon to blue.

Network Rail then followed up with an order for 94 further Tiphook KPA conversions, which were conducted by Wabtec at Doncaster and completed by the summer of 2001, with sets initially recorded working from Basford Hall, Temple Mills, Rugby, and Millerhill. These were to the same specification as the previous ten with one generator wagon per five vehicles and again coded JJA.

ABOVE: When first converted, the prototype autoballaster 83 70 6905 048-7 retained its end ladder while a Transrail 'T' logo was applied to the hopper sides. Still TOPS coded KPA, it received the new design code of E833 and, together with two other Tiphook wagons, was then sent on tour to various yards around the country. However, when recorded at Tees Yard in February 1997 with the next nine conversions, it had lost both the Transrail logo and the end ladder. Mark Saunders

High capacity upgrades

The KPA donor wagons included a number of examples that had seen their hopper ends cut down earlier in their careers in order to fit under loading equipment at Peak Forest and this feature remained unchanged on becoming autoballasters, although they were in the minority. The Railtrack conversions were all finished in beige with a broad blue band and white lettering, taking the numbers GERS12911-99 and GERS13001-05. Notably, the ten original autoballasters converted in 1995/96 were reworked as part of the Railtrack order, emerging as GERS12990/92-99 and GERS13001.

New build

The success of the design also prompted Railtrack to order a batch of new autoballasters from Wabtec, with 38 five-wagon sets being delivered in the final months of 2001. Unlike the conversions, which retained their Y25C bogies, the 190 new autoballasters were fitted with ABC-NACO Axle-Motion III track-friendly bogies and coded HQA on TOPS. In addition, knuckle couplings were fitted within each five-wagon set with buffers and screw couplings only provided on the outer ends of the outer wagons.

The HQAs were numbered 380001-038 for the outers, 380301-380338 for outers with a generator and 380101-214 for the inners. The inner wagons also featured modified discharge chutes which had a hinged flap to extend the throw of the ballast during discharge if required. All of the HQAs also featured cleaner solebars without the plated over door actuator holes that could be found on the JJAs, while they could all carry 64.3 tonnes, apart from the generator wagons where the payload was reduced to 60.8 tonnes.

The initial use of the HQAs was to carry stone from ARC's Machen Quarry to the Channel Tunnel Rail Link construction site at Beechbrook Farm, Ashford, and also work on the tracklaying of the high speed line itself. When this role was concluded in 2004, they joined the JJA autoballasters in the nationwide Network Rail pool.

The other nine initial autoballaster conversions, which were all taken from the second batch of Tiphook KPA hoppers built in 1990, were allocated to design code E839, with 83 70 6905 173-3 recorded at Longport on May 23, 1999. The GTRM logo had been added after the set was hired to the infrastructure maintenance company. *David Ratcliffe*

Additional sets

A further ten HQA five-wagon sets were built by Wabtec in late 2003 and delivered in all-over yellow with large Network Rail logos. Otherwise similar to the earlier HQAs, they were numbered 380401-410 for outers with a generator, 380501-510 for outers and 380601-630 for inners.

Wabtec produced a final build of ten autoballaster wagons for GB Railfreight in mid-2006, these being numbered as 380701/06 outers with generators, 380702-04/07-09 inners and 380705/10 outers. These two five-wagons sets were finished in Metronet yellow and lettered 'Metronet Renewing the Tube' complete with Metronet, GBRf and London Underground logos. They were initially used on the newly awarded Metronet track renewal contract and could be seen invariably working together on the open-air sections of the Metropolitan and District lines from their operating base at Wellingborough Yard.

Now an autoballaster support wagon, former Tiphook 'piggyback' KOA 83 70 4798 054-0 was also at Longport in May 1999. Carrying a generator and a compressor, this wagon allowed the initial autoballaster set to operate independently of a locomotive's air supply. *David Ratcliffe*

Modelling BR: Engineers Wagons of Privatisation 67

High capacity upgrades

ABOVE: Displaying the original look of the Railtrack JJAs, GERS12912 waits for the weekend in Westbury Down Yard on September 12, 2002. The four rectangular plates show where the original hopper door actuators were, these being plated over upon conversion to autoballasters. These are only found on the JJAs, making them easy to tell apart from HQAs. *David Ratcliffe*

From 2007, the HQAs and JJAs in beige and blue began to have the obsolete Railtrack lettering obscured beneath rectangular blue patches with Network Rail logos then added on top from 2009 onwards. The next change came in mid-2010 when last built GERS13001-05 were renumbered as GERS12895-99, putting them at the beginning of the number series instead.

Early in 2016, Network Rail took ownership of all the JJAs, a programme to re-prefix 12895-99 and 12901-99 from GERS to NR beginning immediately to denote the change. At the same time, a partial rebranding was conducted with the upper blue band being replaced by a yellow one, again with a Network Rail logo. This programme was completed on all JJAs by the spring of 2017 and included the ten former GTRM/Carillion wagons. In contrast, none of the HQAs have received this cosmetic change, all of the first batch continuing to operate in beige/blue while the later build remains in yellow, albeit increasingly lost beneath rust and grime.

Operations
The autoballasters have always been used to deliver new top ballast from both actual and virtual quarries to worksites across the rail network, and with a fleet of only 354 vehicles they see intensive use with the majority in action most weekends. With the HQAs formed into fixed rakes of five, they are only ever seen in multiples of this with five, ten, 15 and 20 wagon formations all commonplace and often top and tailed. Longer sets can operate if required, the construction of the Borders Rail Link seeing 30 wagon autoballaster rakes at work for example.

The JJAs invariably operate in the same multiples of five manner nowadays, although as they all have conventional drawgear, it has been possible to note six wagon formations or multiples thereof in the past, while the generator wagon can be anywhere in the set. On occasions, formations of less than five JJAs have been noted but these are usually transiting to or from maintenance. The two autoballaster types can also be seen together in the same trains in their sets of five.

ABOVE: Several of the Tiphook donor hoppers had the top of their ends cut down to the height of the sides in the early 1990s, and these were among the KPAs converted into autoballasters. GERS13003, with modified hinged discharge chutes, is pictured at Crewe Gresty Lane on January 23, 2005. Five years later, this wagon would be renumbered as GERS12897. *David Ratcliffe*

ABOVE: Originally delivered with GTRM branding, JJA GERS12906 shows off its revised Carillion logo at Basford Hall on April 21, 2012. By now, this batch of ten autoballasters had passed to the lease of Network Rail and would transfer to its ownership with the rest of the fleet in 2016. *Dan Adkins*

High capacity upgrades

RIGHT: Rows of nearly new HQA autoballasters rest for the weekend at Beechbrook Farm in September 2002 while engaged on the construction of the Channel Tunnel Rail Link. Taking centre stage is generator-fitted 380319, the cover over the opposite end protecting the air brake equipment. In the background are hired-in Class 20s 20142 and 20188, which were normally deployed on the lightweight wiring trains. Once the line was completed, this entire site was returned to green fields. Simon Bendall

LEFT: The generator fitted to the autoballasters is sizeable as is the canopy that protects it, as demonstrated by HQA outer 380314 at Kingsthorpe on August 26, 2017. Like the JJAs, the purpose-built HQAs were delivered with Railtrack branding but this was later obscured beneath a blue patch and then a Network Rail logo added on top. The large '04' dates from the wagon's time on constructing the Channel Tunnel Rail Link when the HQAs were formed into longer rakes, each with their own set number. Dan Adkins

BELOW: Unusually, the HQAs carry the fourth letter of their TOPS code, something that is not often seen, and which has been updated once during their lives. Inner 380111 has knuckle couplings and no buffers at both ends, as shown at Crewe on April 15, 2019. Each of the discharge chutes can be remotely controlled to enable precision positioning of the ballast, which can be dropped when the wagon is traveling at up to 10 mph. David Ratcliffe

High capacity upgrades

ABOVE: The final batch of HQAs for Network Rail were delivered in the company's yellow livery, as shown by a still relatively clean 380609 at Basford Hall on June 9, 2005. As an inner wagon, it has knuckle couplings at both ends, which are finished in yellow as well, while the fold down extensions to the discharge chutes can also be seen. David Ratcliffe

LEFT: Due to the condition of their bodywork, the yellow HQAs received fresh Network Rail logos around 2015, the yellow patch obscuring the original with the white-backed replacement showing up better. As ever, rust is much in evidence on the intensively used wagons as 380609 rolls through Kings Norton on August 17, 2015, ten years after the previous image. Dan Adkins

RIGHT: The last batch of autoballasters for UK use were ordered by GB Railfreight for the Metronet contract. On February 28, 2007, a brand new 380707 was on display at Wansford, this showing the many company logos carried by the Metronet fleet as well as the lemony shade of yellow employed. These wagons still work for GBRf today and are often to be found south of the Thames but in far less showroom condition! Gareth Bayer

70 www.keymodelworld.com

High capacity upgrades

LEFT: All of the JJAs received a partial re-livery and new number prefix in 2016/17 after their acquisition by Network Rail following the sale of GE Rail Services to Touax, this including a black company logo. The rest of the wagons remained in dirty and rusty beige though. On May 23, 2018, NR12949 was pictured returning to Crewe after working in a possession near Watford Junction. David Ratcliffe

RIGHT: The ten former GTRM/Carillion autoballasters were included in the Network Rail rebranding as NR12909 shows at Kingsthorpe on August 26, 2017. The size of the yellow panel applied to the re-liveried JJAs varied across the fleet and in this case had failed to cover the previous livery's upper and lower blue stripes. Dan Adkins

One of Network Rail's core infrastructure services on weekdays runs between Hoo Junction in Kent and Whitemoor Yard. Now powered by GB Railfreight, the service was previously part of the Colas portfolio and on October 31, 2014, 70810 and 70807 near their destination as they pass through March with the 6L37 northbound working. On this occasion, the load was a set of five HQA autoballasters. Timara Easter

Modelling BR: Engineers Wagons of Privatisation 71

High capacity upgrades

A dirty autoballaster

Network Rail's autoballaster fleet has seen intensive use for over two decades, this taking a toll on their appearance. Mike Cubberley describes how he weathered one of Bachmann's OO gauge models using a mix of enamels and acrylics.

Like all wagons of this type, sitting around between possessions allows the British weather to have an impact with a basic rust-coloured patina developing and tinged with some lighter ballast dust as a final layer. The loading of these wagons with front loader buckets allows the top of the body to be dashed with spilt stone, which produces a closely grouped pattern of spot damage to the paintwork over time.

Stippling with a stiff paint brush is one of the best methods to create the base layer for this weathering effect. Working from photos shows that you need to produce an inverted shallow crescent with the low point in the centre of the top third of the body. This is best done using a dark colour, such as track weathering brown, working slowly and in a couple of passes.

After allowing this to dry fully, the layering of colours can start. Each layer needs to be slightly lighter and heading towards the more orangey finish of newer rust. A series of thin acrylic washes will allow you to do this quiet easily. Have a pot of the correct thinners and/or water to hand and work down the bodysides with a wide flat brush. Once you are happy with the wash opacity and colouration, leave it to dry thoroughly, although using acrylics allows this to be a fairly quick process.

Underframe dirt

Looking at the solebars, the main shade is usually a combination of track colour and light rust washed down the body and built up against any raised surfaces. Once the brown washes are applied, you can add mid and dark grey highlight washes on the horizontal surfaces.

The end protection plates and canopy roof have tended to end up in the same track brown colour and this seems to be quite uniform in its coverage. A couple of layers of dark to mid tone track/rusty browns will do the trick, this being painted on with a flat brush across the panels side to side. The ends of the hoppers have tended to stay fairly clean, and it is best to just wash over

ABOVE: By building up layers of different colours, the well-used look of the autoballasters can be created, this incorporating shades of rust, track dirt and ballast dust.

these areas. The walkways and handrails also need a wash using the same colours from the solebars, trying to get under the end covers as much as possible.

Less is always more so frequent stops for a break allows the washes to dry off a bit and your finished JJA slowly appears before you. The bogies and underframe chutes should be worked over with a suitable brown and the inside of the chutes painted in the same order of colours that the hopper body was, namely dark to light. A final lighter orange colour can then be added before a gentle dry brush of a light grey to give a dusty look to the surface of the chutes. The last task is to apply a few light coats of matt varnish to seal and bring together the various shades and finishes.

ABOVE: If looking to produce an autoballaster with its Railtrack lettering obscured, Railtec produces the blue patches in transfer form for 2mm and 4mm, both with and without Network Rail logos incorporated. The company also offers renumbering packs.

High capacity upgrades

ABOVE: After a long absence, this year has seen Bachmann's models of the JJA autoballasters reappear in both N and OO. In both cases, the new releases are finished in the current look for the wagons with yellow replacing the blue band and black logos applied on top. They also have a weathered finish that includes a representation of chipped paint around the hopper aperture, on the discharge chutes and on the cover plates over the generator and brake equipment. The 2mm models are exclusively available from Rails of Sheffield with the generator wagon produced alongside both round and flat-topped standard JJAs. In 4mm, just the generator and round-topped versions have been released and the duo are only available from the Bachmann Collectors' Club.

ABOVE: When ballasting has been required on one of the lines in the Scottish Highlands, this has tended to be done in one hit with a set of autoballasters spending a week or so based in the area with reloading taking place at a suitable location. George Woodcock's OO gauge model of Georgemas Junction recreates this operation with a set of JJAs being resupplied from the loading platform. Dennis Taylor

LEFT: Whereas the HQA variant of the autoballasters is unavailable in OO gauge, those working in 2mm can enjoy the N Gauge Society kit, which allows the yellow-liveried sets to be accurately modelled. This is particularly apparent on the Epsom & Ewell Model Railway Club's recreation of Hinksey Yard, which is based on the infrastructure yard located to the south of Oxford station. In this view, 97302 passes the virtual quarry and yellow HQAs with a set of JJAs. Timara Easter

Modelling BR: Engineers Wagons of Privatisation 73

GREAT SUBSCRIPTION OFFERS FROM

SUBSCRIBE
TO *YOUR* FAVOURITE MAGAZINE
AND SAVE

News, Views and Analysis on Today's Railway

Established for 50 years, Modern Railways has earned its reputation in the industry as a highly respected railway journal. Providing in-depth coverage of all aspects of the industry, from traction and rolling stock to signalling and infrastructure management, Modern Railways carries the latest news alongside detailed analysis, making it essential reading for industry professionals and railway enthusiasts alike.

modernrailways.com

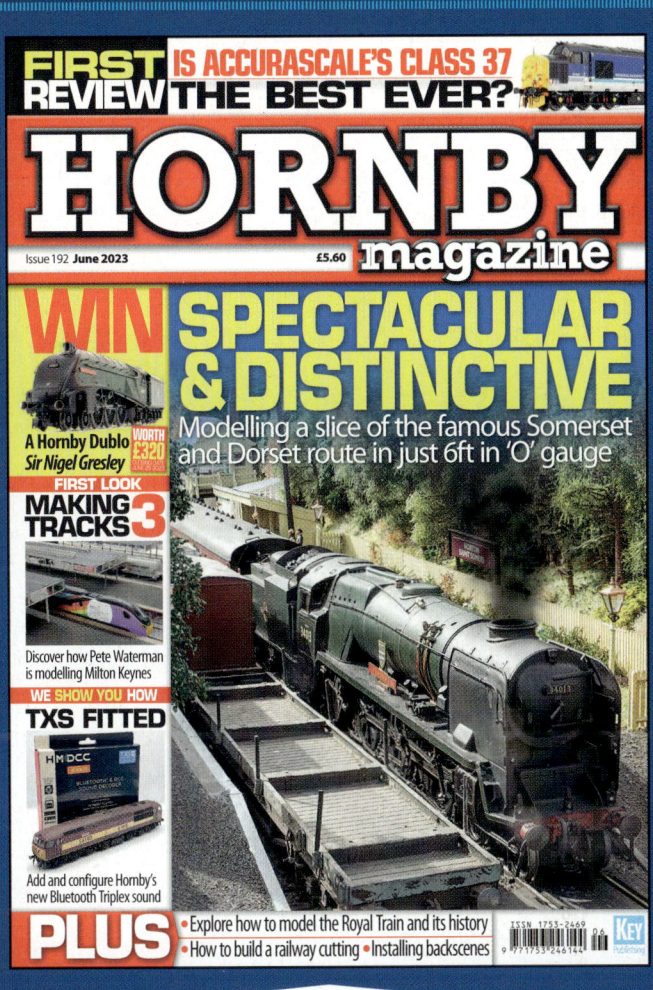

Written by modellers, for modellers...

Hornby Magazine takes a unique approach to model railways with both the relatively inexperienced and the seasoned modeller in mind. Unique step-by-step guides offer modellers hints and tips on how to get the most from the hobby. The very best photography and all the very latest news inspire and inform modellers of all abilities. Hornby Magazine is dedicated to promoting this most rewarding of hobbies, introducing it to newcomers and those returning to the hobby.

Keymodelworld.com/Hornby-magazine

FOR THE LATEST SUBSCRIPTION DEALS

VISIT:
www.keypublishing.com/shop

PHONE:
(UK) **01780 480404** • (Overseas) **+44 1780 480404**

High capacity upgrades

MCA/MDA ballast opens

The MCA/MDA were the unplanned result of EWS building too many MBA 'monster boxes' that then failed to find employment. However, their conversion created the 'gondola' ballast wagon that still serves as the template for orders today. **Simon Bendall** looks at their careers.

ABOVE: Crewe is one of the best places to see the MCA/MDA fleet as they have been associated with West Coast workings for over two decades. On June 9, 2005, last built MDA 500300 rests in Basford Hall with a load of fresh ballast. The MDAs are inner wagons with no conventional drawgear whatsoever, only fixed AAR auto-couplings. *David Ratcliffe*

One of the highlights of EWS' wagon building programme at the turn of the century was the appearance of the MBA 'monster boxes' from the Thrall workshops at York. Aptly named, the big maroon boxes were some of the largest wagons to be seen on the network when they debuted in the spring of 1999 and went on to find employment on aggregates and scrap workings in particular.

However, for many traffics, the MBAs were just too big, and EWS struggled to fully utilise the 300 wagons that had been built. The very high sides were also an issue with a number of terminals lacking mechanical grabs that were tall enough for the operator to see properly. Therefore, with the wagons only a year old, EWS announced that a third of the fleet, 100 wagons, would be returned to York to be substantially cut down to around a third of the original height.

The final 100 MBAs, 500201-300, were selected for rebuilding with the work commencing in the autumn of 2000. Two new TOPS codes were assigned on completion with 500201-240 becoming MCAs while 500241-300 appeared as MDAs. The MCAs were outer wagons with buffers at both ends along with swing-head auto-couplings and a standard coupling hook behind, while the MDAs were inners with no buffers or coupling hooks and just fixed AAR buckeyes.

All of the rebuilds had been completed by the autumn of 2001 and while a mixed commodity use had initially been envisaged, the 100 wagons were dedicated to ballast and spoil work, particularly on the modernisation of the West Coast Main Line initially. Typically, they were formed in five wagon sets with three MDAs sandwiched between an MCA at each end.

This deployment on main lines has remained a trait of the design ever since, being often seen working on the West Coast, Midland, and East Coast routes from the likes of Bescot, Crewe, Toton, Doncaster, and Tyne Yard. They have seen some use on virtual quarry circuits, the Stud Farm-Westbury flow bringing them to the former Western Region for example. In contrast, they are comparatively rare on the Southern, although they have reached Eastleigh on occasions with inter-regional workings from Hinksey and Westbury. Aside from the painting out of the EWS lettering, the MCA/MDA have remained unchanged since conversion with the maroon livery now buried beneath layers of dirt. They have acquired a codename over the years though, this being Swordfish.

ABOVE: Now more brown than maroon, MCA 500231 brings up the rear of the 7R01 Bescot-North Wembley Junction infrastructure service at Kingsthorpe on April 9, 2016. The MCAs have buffers at both ends along with the swinghead variety of auto-coupler for use with EWS/DB Class 66s. When other traction is required to haul the wagons, this can be swung to the side to give access to a conventional coupling hook. *Dan Adkins*

High capacity upgrades

RIGHT: The clean patch left by the removal or painting out of the EWS lettering can be seen in the middle of the wagon as MDA 500241 heads south at Ribblehead on August 26, 2021, in the consist of the 6K05 Carlisle Yard-Basford Hall. David Ratcliffe

ABOVE: Using the MCA coupling hook, Freightliner's 66539 brings a long rake of MCA/MDA through Daresbury on April 9, 2017, while forming a 6Y56 Golborne Junction-Basford Hall loaded spoil. Under the Network Rail contracts held by the freight companies, it is common to see locos from one operator hauling wagons belonging to another. Mark Latham

MCA/MDA models

While both Bachmann and Dapol have produced the MBA ready-to-run in OO gauge, only Dapol opted to do the cut-down MCA/MDA variant as well, Bachmann instead plumping for the closely related MOA. However, like the MRA side-tippers, there has not been a batch of the ballast wagons from Dapol for some years, making them hard to come by. Some 20 years or so ago, Hurst Models offered a very nice resin kit for the wagons along with a comprehensive transfer sheet to complete the job, although this is now equally rare. Still, it is better than the options available in N where a RTR MCA/MDA has yet to appear.

ABOVE: The Dapol MCA/MDA was perhaps a little on the chunky side when first released but still it fulfilled a need and is another of the manufacturer's range to have seemingly disappeared.

ABOVE: The 4mm scale Hurst Models kit featured a one-piece resin body with etched and whitemetal details, it took longer to apply the myriad of transfers than it did to assemble!

Modelling BR: Engineers Wagons of Privatisation 77

High capacity upgrades

LEFT: With fresh ballast on board, 500343 rolls through Water Orton behind 66755 on April 15, 2016, while heading up the 6G16 Stud Farm-Bescot. The design is virtually indistinguishable from the earlier MCA/MDA conversions besides the drawgear.
Dan Adkins

MOA ballast opens

Largely identical to the MCA/MDA, the small fleet of MOA were from a European-built follow on order that has surprisingly seen ready-to-run production in two scales. **Simon Bendall** casts an eye over them.

Despite the unplanned nature of the MCA/MDA conversions, they proved to be sufficiently successful to warrant a follow on order by EWS in 2003. However, with Thrall having now closed its facility at York Works due to lack of orders, these additional wagons were built at the Trinity/Thrall workshops in the Czech Republic.

Classified as MOAs, the resulting 50-strong fleet was all but identical to the MCA/MDA, the main alteration being the abandonment of the auto-couplers in favour of fitting buffers and screw couplings at both ends. The numbering followed on from their predecessors as 500301-350 with EWS maroon again carried. Most of the wagons reached the UK in May 2003 and they were at work alongside the MCA/MDA within a couple of months, again carrying ballast and spoil in conjunction with the West Coast Route Modernisation project.

Since then, the MOAs have spread their wings in the same manner and are typically found mixed in with the MCA/MDA sets, either operating as five-wagon rakes themselves or in smaller amounts to allow trains to be lengthened. Five wagon sets have also been noted out on their own at times.

MOA models

It is perhaps slightly surprising that Bachmann opted to tool up the MOA for ready to run production in both its N and OO gauge ranges given the MCAs are better known, but doubtless their ability to run as individual wagons played a part.

A nice job was certainly made of the OO gauge model with the brake rigging strung beneath the box body and lots of separate parts. As supplied in the box, they feature working buckeye couplings at both ends, although these are not fitted to the real things, with standard tension locks in the accessory bag. The same can be said of the Farish rendering, the models just requiring some weathering to make them look properly authentic.

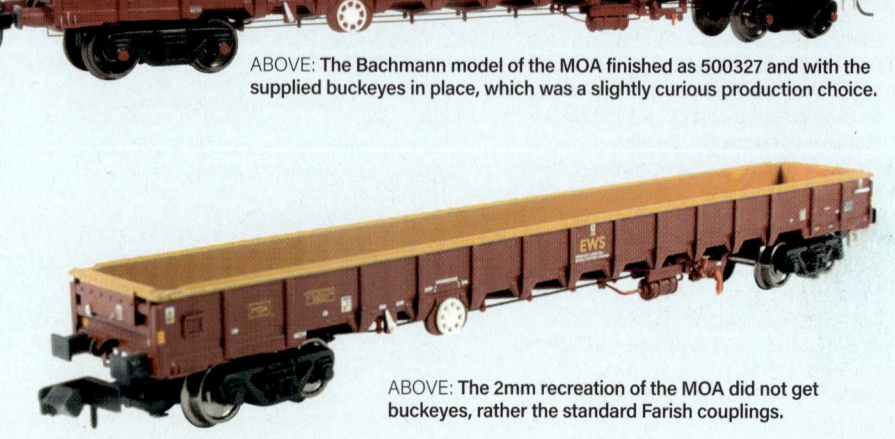

ABOVE: The Bachmann model of the MOA finished as 500327 and with the supplied buckeyes in place, which was a slightly curious production choice.

ABOVE: The 2mm recreation of the MOA did not get buckeyes, rather the standard Farish couplings.

High capacity upgrades

JNA ballast opens

The Falcons were the first of the long 'gondola' style ballast wagons to be acquired by Network Rail, seeing off many of the inherited ex BR types. Now approaching 20 years old, they continue to be a key component of the company's infrastructure fleet. **Simon Bendall** looks at their history.

While dirty, JNA Falcon NLU29011 was still in respectable condition on October 13, 2012, with no graffiti and little in the way of bodyside scarring. The wagon is seen alongside DRS' Crewe Gresty Bridge depot during a shunt move out of Basford Hall. Simon Bendall

One of Network Rail's first significant investments in engineers' stock following its creation in 2002 was a fleet of bogie opens suitable for both ballast and spoil work. Built by Trinity Rail at its Astra Vagoane workshops in Romania, a total of 555 JNAs were delivered to the UK between November 2003 and May 2004. Numbered in the private owner series as NLU29001-555 (the NLU standing for National Logistics Unit), the design quickly acquired the codename of Falcon in the same manner as the various fish-related designations.

Riding on NACO Axle Motion III bogies and with a gross laden weight of 90 tonnes and 60mph maximum speed, the wagons were a development of the earlier MCA/MDA and MOA designs operated by EWS and later DB. Acquired as part of Network Rail's modernisation of its infrastructure fleet, the Falcons offered a step change in capacity and reliability. Their deployment had an immediate impact on several of the inherited ex BR fleets, including the ZBA Rudds and MGV/ZCV Clams, while the ZCA Sea Urchins also suffered numerous casualties, both from the BR builds and those converted by Mainline, Transrail and EWS.

The new order was soon seen operating nationwide, carrying both new ballast to worksites and removing spoil, while they have also been noted loaded with recovered sleepers. As well as possession duties, the Falcons have been regularly deployed on virtual quarry workings over the years, particularly before the arrival of the IOA bulk ballast boxes.

Mixed formations

With the arrival of further ballast wagon types, the JNAs have become mixed together with the MLAs and the IEAs, all being to the same basic design. They have also worked alongside the various two-axle EWS-owned box wagons and rail and sleeper carriers. Train lengths can vary from a handful of wagons to long strings as required while, cosmetically, many now sport patch painting to cover up the graffiti acquired over the past two decades, normally in a different shade of yellow.

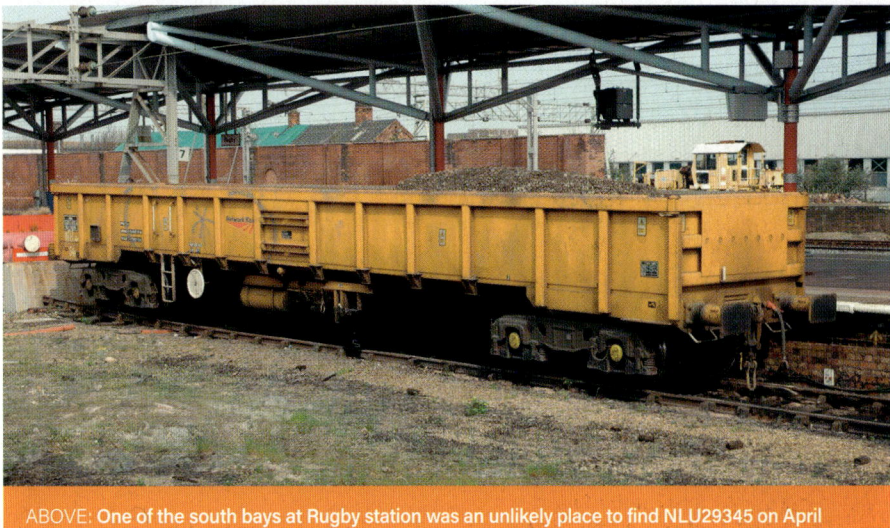

ABOVE: One of the south bays at Rugby station was an unlikely place to find NLU29345 on April 23, 2007. Well loaded with spoil, the wagon had presumably been cut out of a passing service with a defect and dumped in the nearest convenient place to await recovery. It would certainly be something a little different to add to a model of a suitably sized station. Simon Bendall

Modelling BR: Engineers Wagons of Privatisation 79

High capacity upgrades

ABOVE: The footbridge over Hinksey Yard, Oxford, has long offered a useful vantage point, especially if seeking internal views of ballast wagons. Around a year old on May 6, 2005, NLU29426 displays a mix of rust and ballast dust on its inside while showing that such wagons are rarely completely empty as grabs cannot get every last piece of ballast out. The same goes for the MKA Limpets alongside with the Falcon also having damp patches on its floor. *David Ratcliffe*

Quite possibly the smartest Falcon on the network today is NLU29024, which was modified at High Marnham during 2014 to be part of Network Rail's High Output Plant System (HOPS), this being the Windhoff-built Multi-Purpose Vehicles purchased to conduct the electrification of the Great Western Main Line. The wagon was assigned to work with the excavation set, where it was to be loaded with spoil and debris while the MPV was conducting lineside preparations, although it did not see a lot of use, if any.

The modifications included adding through cabling so it could be formed in between MPV vehicles, installation of solebar lighting, fitting of tail lights at one end only, and a full repaint in yellow. It emerged from the process without Network Rail logos. Originally, it was due to be renumbered as 99 70 9131 007-5 but this identity was never applied. Following completion of the project, it was returned to normal traffic in 2018 after the reversal of all its modifications. However, its different shade of yellow and lack of logos ensures it still stands out as something a little different.

In terms of models, Dapol has cornered the market here with recreations of the JNA Falcons in both N and OO, the latter being weathered and graffitied overleaf. Both have seen numerous production runs so a decent length set can be assembled without any need for renumbering.

LEFT: With Trinity Rail having previously acquired Thrall, it was no great surprise that the JNA Falcons shared a number of design similarities with the earlier MCA/MDA/MOA designs. This included the reinforced access door in the centre of the bodysides to allow sweeping out and the ribbed ends with a steel plate bridging across them. NLU29245 enjoys the winter sun at Crewe Gresty Lane in January 2005. *David Ratcliffe*

RIGHT: Newly released from its modifications, NLU29024 stands at the Swindon base of the High Output Plant System on March 21, 2014, in ex-works yellow. The two tail lights added to one end are clear to see while the lights and silver conduit fitted beneath the body can also be glimpsed. Also notable is the emergency stop button by the buffer in addition to other fittings. These were all removed when it reverted to a standard ballast wagon. *Rich Martin*

High capacity upgrades

ABOVE: Spring had arrived at Red Bank, near Newton-le-Willows, on April 24, 2016, as the pioneer low-emission Class 66, 66951, powers along with a Basford Hall to Carnforth working bound for a weekend possession. Three JNA Falcons are marshalled behind the Freightliner machine followed by a small number of EWS two-axle boxes and a long rake of bogie opens, including numerous Falcons and a few MLAs. Mark Latham

ABOVE: The Falcons are perhaps the modern equivalent of the Rudds or Grampus, getting everywhere and carrying a range of loads while being hauled by an array of motive power. Colas Rail's 56113 had charge of 13 bogie opens loaded with spoil on July 12, 2020, at Standish while forming a 6C92 Carnforth-Basford Hall service. The seven JNA Falcons ae easily distinguishable thanks to their more golden shade of yellow while the five MLAs and solitary IEA stand out in their brighter yellow or EWS maroon. Mark Latham

ABOVE: Illustrating the kind of shorter formation that a JNA Falcon can sometimes be found in, a solitary example was making up the consist of the 6K05 Carlisle Yard-Basford Hall on November 26, 2020, along with four MHAs. The latter comprise one of the original batch with 16 bodyside ribs and three of the later 11-rib versions, all carrying sand. Providing the power on the approach to Settle Junction were 68017 *Hornet* and 68016 *Fearless*. Mark Latham

Modelling BR: Engineers Wagons of Privatisation **81**

High capacity upgrades

JNA NLU29064 displays the distinctive graffiti on two panels along with a variety of associated tags.

A life of grime

While it may not be to many people's tastes, graffiti is an unavoidable sight on the modern railway and today's high capacity wagons are particularly tempting targets due to their large expanses of bodywork. **Mick Bryan** describes how to weather and 'tag' a rake of Dapol's JNA Falcon ballast wagons.

When the Dapol JNA Falcon was first released back in 2010, initial impressions were that the yellow finish looked too 'plasticky' and that the bogies lacked depth. However, with a little weathering, these ubiquitous Network Rail ballast wagons can be quickly transformed into a highly useful model, particularly bringing out the moulding on the bogies.

The basic weathering was created by airbrushing the wagon all over with layers of track dirt and brake dust. Before it was fully dry, a cotton bud damped with thinners was used to remove some of the paint on the body panels, leaving dirtier areas in the corners. More weathering was applied using dry brushing and additional airbrushing to create the look of individual wagons. The interior can also be treated with rust colours while areas such as the handbrake wheels and steps should be kept largely clean as per the real thing.

Some of the body panels can be over-painted with fresh yellow to represent wagons where repairs or painting out of graffiti has taken place. Further light weathering of the repainted panels can then also be added. The maxim of 'less is more' is definitely worth following as the layers are built up.

Recreating reality

While photographing JNAs being used on engineering work near my house, I had a chance to snap a few decent reference

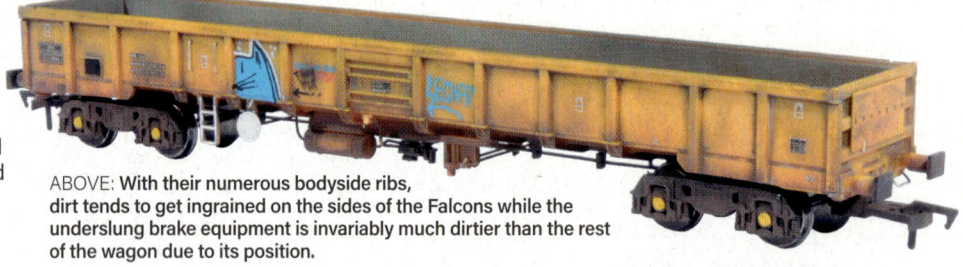

ABOVE: With their numerous bodyside ribs, dirt tends to get ingrained on the sides of the Falcons while the underslung brake equipment is invariably much dirtier than the rest of the wagon due to its position.

ABOVE: The inspiration for the first graffitied JNA Falcon, NLU29348 stands at Langho, near Blackburn, during engineering work in November 2008. Heavily loaded with ballast, the Falcons have proved to be highly useful wagons for Network Rail and can be found across the UK. *Mick Bryan*

ABOVE: Comparing the model with the photo shows how the graffiti has been recreated in miniature by painting freehand and building up the layers of colour.

High capacity upgrades

photographs and one of them was carrying a 'Le Chat' graffiti tag. Graffiti is an unavoidable aspect of the present day, especially where any large flat surface is available, and railway vehicles often provide the canvas for this unwelcome form of self-expression.

Although transfers are available to represent graffiti, I wanted something different and as I am a cat-lover, 'Le Chat' appealed to me so I decided to have a go. I did consider using the photographs and printing onto transfer paper, but these may not have worked well over the various bodyside ribs. An advantage of hand painting is that if I made a serious mistake, I could always patch paint it with yellow and start again!

As with weathering, I practised on a couple of old bodyshells that we all seem to have lurking at the bottom of the stock drawer. The 'tag' area was marked out with faint pencil lines and then filled in using suitable shades of enamel or acrylic with a very fine brush and steady hand. The image was built up from the inside out, starting with the main body of paint and finishing off with the outline and detail. For some of the black wording and fine lines, I used a very fine permanent marker pen.

To create the illusion of a spray can finish, the edges of the painted areas were finished off with very small amounts of paint on the brush. This was done by dipping the brush in the paint as normal and then wiping off the excess on a small piece of cloth. Not quite 'dry-brushing' but more 'damp-brushing'.

I posted a picture of the first completed wagon on a couple of model railway internet forums and, as a result, I was sent a few more pictures of suitably graffitied JNAs, including another 'Le Chat' and 'Soak'. I was also fortunate to find another 'Le Chat' myself, which I have since copied in model form. The most recent picture sent to me is of a JNA with a 'Le Chat' shaped patch of recently applied yellow paint!

ABOVE: **The largest of the cat-themed tags to be recreated covers more than two panels, necessitating some careful work over the ribs.**

ABOVE AND RIGHT: **A different style applied to NLU29012, created by first applying the basic white shapes and then adding the black detail with a fine brush and finally the red outline.**

ABOVE: **Dapol produces the JNA Falcon in N gauge as well as OO, the manufacturer having produced several batches of both over the years, ensuring there are plenty of running numbers to choose from.**

Modelling BR: Engineers Wagons of Privatisation 83

High capacity upgrades

With the Metronet contract long concluded, the brandings on MLA 503045 were rather obsolete as it passed Didcot Yard on October 1, 2011, with a backdrop of the DB servicing depot, Thames Valley signalling centre and the now demolished power station. The bodyside hatch fitted to 503001-090 can be seen on the nearest end. *Brian Daniels*

MLA ballast opens

The next development in the series of bogie ballast boxes was this Greenbrier-built design, it found favour not only with Network Rail, but also EWS and GB Railfreight. **Simon Bendall** looks at their evolution.

It was the Metronet contract with GB Railfreight that brought the first order for these low-sided ballast opens, this going to Greenbrier Europe with construction taking place in Poland. Similar in concept to the JNAs, 140 examples coded MLA were ordered with 90 being for GBRf while the other 50 were for Network Rail in exchange for 25 MRA side-tippers.

Deliveries commenced in the early summer of 2006 with 503001-090 being delivered to the centre of Metronet operations at Wellingborough Yard while 503091-140 followed immediately afterwards for Network Rail, the latter being deployed into ballast and spoil traffic.

Notable differences on the MLAs compared to the Trinity Rail-built JNAs were straight solebars and the use of Y25 bogies, while the right hand end of each bodyside featured a solebar step and three horizontal rungs to give internal access. At the left hand end, the 90 Metronet wagons incorporated a bodyside hatch to allow sweeping out, but this was omitted on the Network Rail batch of 50. All were delivered in yellow with either the suite of Metronet and GBRf brandings or Network Rail logos depending on their owner.

Yellow to maroon
The next order for MLAs came from EWS with Greenbrier Europe constructing 105 examples to support the freight operator's recently awarded seven-year infrastructure contract with Network Rail. 503500-604 were delivered to the UK between February and June 2008, all carrying maroon with yellow top capping, although by now the company was in DB ownership. The bodyside hatch was again omitted while the most significant change was the use of Axle Motion III bogies in place of the previous Y25s. Deployment on ballast workings across the country was immediate and triggered the withdrawal of the remaining ZBA Rudds. These also soon acquired the codename of Red Snapper although, like the other modern names, it was not carried.

In more recent years, the three batches of MLAs have essentially been pooled so can be seen working alongside each other as well as JNA Falcons and IEAs. The maroon on what is now the DB Cargo owned batch has weathered particularly badly with the

ABOVE: A year old 503127 was well loaded with new ballast when stabled at Washwood Heath on June 26, 2007. The difference in the shade of yellow compared to the JNA Falcon to the left is apparent and something that stands out in train formations. *Brian Daniels*

High capacity upgrades

wagons faded to white-tinged pink with a patch of fresher maroon in some cases where the EWS lettering has been painted out. Equally, the Network Rail logos on its MLAs have been bleached out while the Metronet lettering on the GBRf wagons has suffered the usual partial or full removal.

In model terms, in 2010 the MLAs were announced as a forthcoming release by Dapol in OO gauge which would have covered all three liveries and both bogie types, but following management restructuring, the plans were dropped along with other wagon types. As a result, they remain a fairly significant gap in any scale.

ABOVE: An almost new 503500 was captured in Hinksey Yard on May 20, 2008, showing off the Axle Motion III bogies fitted to the EWS order for MLAs. Like the Network Rail batch, these also lacked the bodyside hatch. Rich Martin

RIGHT: When recorded at Northampton on May 3, 2014, 503562 was more of a 'pink snapper' as the fading and whitening of the maroon was already underway and would only get worse. The obsolete EWS lettering had also been removed with the wagon formed in the consist of a 6A13 Bescot-Bourne End Junction loaded ballast. Dan Adkins

LEFT: When recorded in Hinksey Yard on March 21, 2020, 503582 had received a recent repaint into DB red, a somewhat rare occurrence for the company. However, within three years, the MLA was again badly faded. Rich Martin

RIGHT: Major engineering work between Manchester Victoria East Junction and Miles Platting Junction saw all four lines closed for several weeks during 2021, with numerous trainloads of spent ballast being railed to Basford Hall for grading. With the loading of another train almost completed, the ballast in MLA 503568 is carefully levelled off prior to departure from the worksite close to Rochdale Road Bridge on August 2. David Ratcliffe

Modelling BR: Engineers Wagons of Privatisation **85**

High capacity upgrades

IOA ballast boxes

The mainstay of today's virtual quarry services, the stocky yellow boxes ply their trade across the network every weekday with barely a glance. **Simon Bendall** recounts their history while **Timara Easter** distresses the OO gauge Dapol model.

Just over two years old, IOA 31 70 5992 010-6 was still largely in good condition standing alongside Eastleigh station on April 2, 2011. The adjacent virtual quarry is currently supplied from Mountsorrel with GB Railfreight providing the haulage from the East Midlands. Simon Bendall

In January 2007 Network Rail issued an invitation to tender for the supply of new box wagons for its virtual quarry circuits. The company was looking to source a total of 120 wagons with a gross laden weight of 102 tonnes. These would be the first vehicles in this weight category to be owned outright by the company, all previous stock having been leased. The specification called for a vehicle similar to the Thrall-built MBAs but designed specifically for carrying bulk ballast, meaning a shorter length due to the weight involved. The order was duly placed with Greenbrier Europe, construction taking place in Poland.

Ahead of the production wagons arriving, a short-lived but related prototype reached the UK in September 2008 in the form of MJA 502201, this being a single box wagon very similar in design to Freightliner's MJA twin boxes and riding on Axiom Rail TF25 bogies. Finished in all-over yellow, it lacked Network Rail logos but underwent running trials from the Railway Technical Centre at Derby that month.

Delivery of the entire production batch took place during February 2009, no less than 110 of the fleet arriving through the Channel Tunnel in just nine days in a considerable feat of logistics. The previous year had seen the use of traditional TOPS numbers come to an end on wagons following the adoption of new European standards on interoperability, meaning that 12-digit international numbers were now to be displayed. As a result, the new boxes were numbered 31 70 5992 001 to 120 and were assigned the TOPS code of IOA(E).

Their appearance was somewhat different to the MJA prototype as, while to the same broad dimensions, the IOAs sported a substantial capping strip around the upper body, giving them a distinctive appearance. Finished in yellow again, it

ABOVE: Moving forward eight years and 31 70 5992 065-0 was showing the effects of its hard life as it approaches its destination as part of the 6U77 13.42 Mountsorrel-Basford Hall on May 21, 2019. On this day, the 20 ballast boxes were in the care of DRS' 66428, the rake having earlier headed south on its daily circuit for reloading. David Ratcliffe

86 www.keymodelworld.com

High capacity upgrades

was difficult to miss that they were owned by Network Rail with three small logos carried per side.

The IOAs were soon deployed into traffic on the virtual quarry duties, their arrival spelling the end for the PNA Piranhas with Network Rail, all of the VTG-owned low-sided green boxes immediately going off hire and into store at Long Marston. Subsequently, the IOAs gained the code name of Mussel, although this is not carried. Having now notched up 14 years of service, the wagons continue to do the job for which they were built, moving vast quantities of ballast in block formations.

ABOVE: **The IOAs have seen haulage behind traction from all five principal freight operators over the years. Back when Freightliner was more involved in virtual quarry work, 66617 passes Bourton on August 31, 2010, with the 6M22 11.56 Westbury to Stud Farm empties. The uniform rake of around 20-22 wagons is entirely consistent for these workings. The Westbury circuit is nowadays a Colas job and invariably uses a Class 70.** Martin Loader

RIGHT: **Five years later and it was a GB Railfreight machine at the head of the 6M40 11.56 Westbury to Stud Farm working as 66748 dodges shadows and track workers as it powers past Baulking, between Swindon and Didcot, on September 30, 2015. On this occasion, just three IOAs were included in the formation with the remainder being JNA Falcons and MLAs. It has always been relatively unusual to see IOAs mixed with other types but has occurred from time to time and is one of the reasons that Network Rail ordered additional big boxes from Wascosa to increase the number of such wagons available.** Martin Loader

Attacking the Dapol IOA

These high-capacity ballast wagons have become a distinctive sight on the network since 2009, with the Dapol model coming out not long afterwards. The real things did not stay clean for long and soon developed lots of scrapes and dents along the bodysides, resulting in quite a stark change in appearance over the past 14 years. This particular model is part of a long rake owned by a friend and fellow club member with the request to take the plasticky appearance off it and make it look like it had been in revenue-earning service for most of a decade.

The various dents and scrapes were replicated using a scraperboard knife, scratching into the flat areas of the body between the ribs and being fairly brutal about it. However, it is easy to get carried away with this, so photos are an absolute must in terms of a guide, and it pays to be relatively random about it. A wash of Humbrol No. 70 brick red was added next, allowing the paint to get into the bodyside scratches and carefully removing the excess with a cotton bud. Care is needed to make sure you do not remove the paint in the areas you want to simulate paint loss! Once dried, I misted a mix of Humbrol Nos. 62 and 27004 over the whole body, streaked downwards with a flat brush slightly dampened with white spirit. A cotton bud was used again to remove any excess.

The interior needs a considerable amount of toning down, being a mid-grey as supplied. A wash of Humbrol No. 70 again took the edge off, followed by a reasonable amount of MIG 'Europe Dust' powder once the paint had dried. Working upwards to create the dust effect in reverse is a good idea, making sure the entire inside is treated in the process.

Moving to the underframe, the bogies are made from a very shiny black plastic, which desperately needs toning down. Several light passes were made with an airbrush of a dark earthy mix, allowing drying between passes to prevent pooling and paint build-up. The axleboxes were later picked out in warning panel yellow as per the real things. Some of the aforementioned MIG powder was also used on the bogies to give further tonal changes. Finally, further dirt build-up on the underframe with a slightly lighter mix helped tone down the bright yellow considerably. A final waft of dirt across the whole model then melded it all together.

ABOVE: **Attacking a RTR model in this way, even a relatively inexpensive one, will not be to everyone's taste but it recreates the brutal life of the IOAs as they are scraped and banged by grabs while unloading at the virtual quarries.**

ABOVE: **Dapol also produces the IOA in its 2mm scale range, both models having seen a number of releases over the years.** Image courtesy Kernow Model Rail Centre

Modelling BR: Engineers Wagons of Privatisation **87**

High capacity upgrades

IEA ballast opens

Ordered at the same time as the IOAs, these were another variety of low-sided open wagon for possession use. However, as **Simon Bendall** explains, they initially shared the same TOPS designation.

ABOVE: Illustrating the spoil side of their use, IEA 31 70 5892 011-5 passes over the level crossing at Long Eaton on December 7, 2014, while working back to Toton from Flitwick Junction as part of a 6B05 engineers' service. The step and handrails positioned part way along the body to allow the interior to be inspected can be seen by the handbrake wheel while the wagon is bookended by an MLA and JNA. Dan Adkins

At the same time as Network Rail sought expressions of interest for constructing what would become the IOA(E) bulk ballast boxes, it was also looking for a further 55 low-sided 90-tonne GLW wagons to supplement the existing JNA Falcon and MLA fleets. These would again be deployed on possession work, both delivering fresh ballast and removing spoil

The order again went to Greenbrier Europe's Polish workshops with deliveries following on from the IOA(E) during May 2009. Again finished in Network Rail yellow, the resulting wagons were very similar in looks to the previous MLAs, the main 'spotting' difference being the repositioned access step and re-styled handrails part way along the body rather than at one end.

While Network Rail had originally envisaged 55 wagons, in the end only 40 were ordered, these being numbered 31 70 5892 001 to 040. Somewhat surprisingly, their TOPS code upon delivery was IOA(F), only the fourth letter indicating the difference between the two very different types of box wagon. With this unsurprisingly leading to confusion when allocating resources, a new code of IEA(A) was assigned and applied after six months in traffic, and this has been their designation ever since.

In traffic, they are interchangeable with the aforementioned JNAs and MLAs and again are found countrywide, being noted at work from the south of England to Wales and Scotland. However, with just 40 examples spread across the UK, they are greatly outnumbered by the other two types and typically only one or two are seen in a formation. Like the MLAs, they can be referred to as Falcons at times and equally no model currently exists in any scale.

ABOVE: Carrying fresh ballast, IEA 31 70 5892 037-0 passes the staff halt at Hoo Junction as the 6Y48 working from Eastleigh prepares to enter the now predominately infrastructure yard in north Kent on February 16, 2018. On weekdays, there are currently two trips in each direction between the pair of Network Rail facilities, which are contracted to GB Railfreight to operate, normally with a Class 66 or sometimes a pair of unmodified Class 73s. Dan Adkins

MAGAZINE SPECIALS

ESSENTIAL READING FROM KEY PUBLISHING

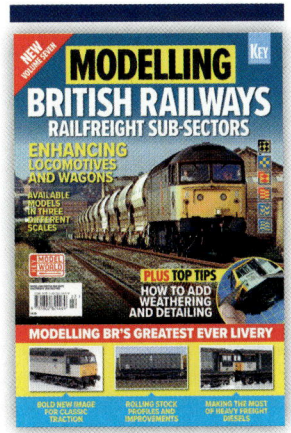
MODELLING BRITISH RAILWAYS
Modelling Railfreight
£8.99 inc FREE P&P*

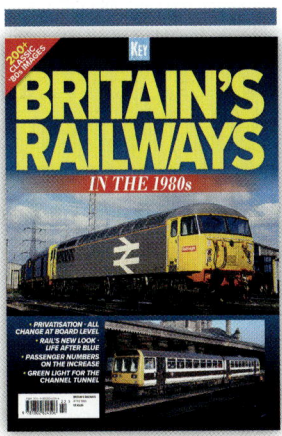
BRITAIN'S RAILWAYS IN THE 1980'S
£8.99 inc FREE P&P*

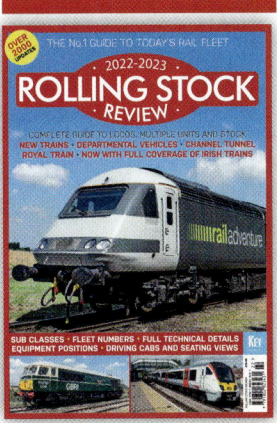
ROLLING STOCK REVIEW 2022/2023
The 212-page title contains almost 2,000 updates compared to the 2021 edition.
£8.99 inc FREE P&P*

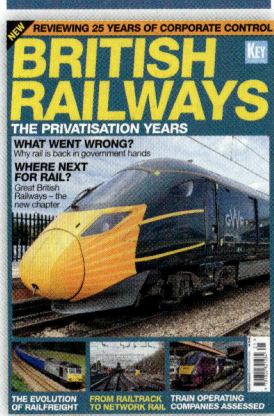
BRITISH RAILWAYS THE PRIVATISATION YEARS
£8.99 inc FREE P&P*

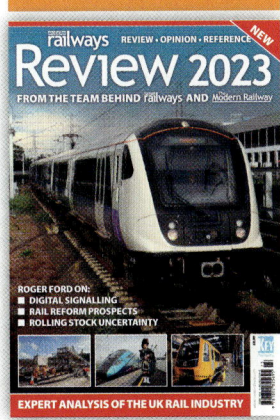
MODERN RAILWAYS REVIEW
The expert editorial team attempts to chart the likely way forward for the year to come.
£8.99 inc FREE P&P*

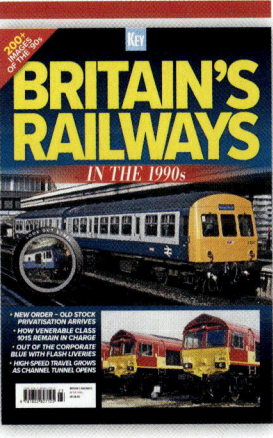
BRITAIN'S RAILWAYS IN THE 1990S
the 90's showed the greatest change in our rail system, with privatisation and booming passenger numbers.
£8.99 inc FREE P&P*

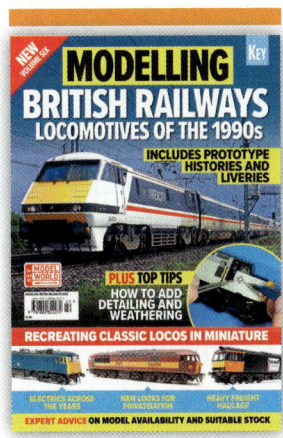
MODELLING BRITISH RAILWAYS
Locomotives of the 1990's
£8.99 inc FREE P&P*

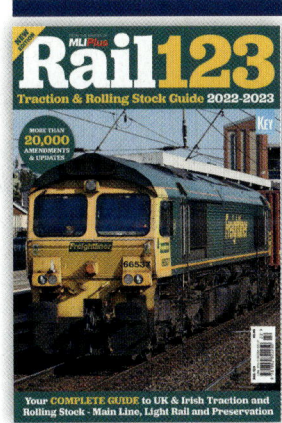
RAIL 123
The only publication to list ALL vehicles in one easy to follow, colour coded list.
£9.99 inc FREE P&P*

MAGAZINE SPECIALS
ESSENTIAL reading from the teams behind your FAVOURITE magazines

HOW TO ORDER

 **VISIT** www.keypublishing.com/shop

 OR

PHONE
UK: 01780 480404
ROW: (+44)1780 480404

*Prices correct at time of going to press. Free 2nd class P&P on all UK & BFPO orders. Overseas charges apply. Postage charges vary depending on total order value.

FREE APP
Simply download to purchase digital versions of your favourite aviation specials in one handy place! Once you have the app, you will be able to download new, out of print or archive specials for less than the cover price!
IN APP ISSUES **£6.99**

A modular future

Recent years have seen Network Rail expand the use of modules for engineering use, building on the experience gained with the likes of the Multi-Purpose Vehicles. There has also been a return to the long engineering tradition of repurposing redundant wagons by putting new bodies on existing chassis. **Simon Bendall** looks at recent trends.

Once they were working properly, the Windhoff Multi-Purpose Vehicles (MPVs) showed what a modular approach to maintenance could deliver, allowing one fleet to be used for several purposes simply by swapping over the equipment carried on their decks. Previously, it had required different vehicles to conduct sandite, de-icing and weedkilling operations at greater expense. Further economies could also be made by using standard vehicles as much as possible and altering their roles as required rather than building bespoke equipment.

The MPV concept was subsequently expanded to create the loco-hauled Railhead Treatment Trains, which used the same modular approach by taking largely standard FEA container flats and fitting them with water tanks, jetting equipment and sandite applicators that could be swapped around as needed, particularly for maintenance.

This idea duly trickled down to the infrastructure wagon fleet where rather than order dedicated new flat wagons to carry track panels, rails and other materials, standard container flats could be procured instead and fitted out with exchangeable decks to perform all of these roles. The upgrading of the London Underground network in the early 2000s was partially the catalyst for the first orders of FEA container flats to carry out such tasks but Network Rail has subsequently followed with the recent delivery of 260 flats in its landmark deal with Wascosa.

New from old

There will always be a need for new ballast wagons, particularly to replace older, lower capacity and more maintenance intensive designs, as illustrated by the remainder of the Wascosa order for both high and low-sided boxes. However, the railway has a long tradition of repurposing old stock for new roles, none more so than for engineering jobs. For a time, this looked to be dying out as operators favoured new stock and the supply of suitable donors started to dry up.

Happily, the practice has undergone a revival in recent years, no doubt influenced by tightening budgets and the need to make the best of what is already to hand. DB Cargo led the way with its rebodying of redundant steel wagons by fitting new bodies to create the unmistakable Lobster fleet and now Network Rail is part way through a similar programme to make better use of its MRA side-tippers. Here too, everything above the chassis has been dispensed with in favour of a sturdy box as the system will never stop needing ballast, no matter how much modernisation goes on.

There is still innovation to be seen though, the past decade bringing the appearance of the Kirow switch and crossing carriers, whose tilting deck allows points to be delivered to worksites already largely assembled and reduce the amount of time needed for installation. The giant vacuum cleaners known as RailVacs have also proven a success, allowing for precision ballast replacement around points and dealing with drainage problems among other tasks, showing that a mix of new technology and old fashioned railway engineering can still co-exist.

Network Rail's newest fleet of ballast wagons are the JNA(Y), which use the underframes of MRA side tippers with a new box body on top. Conversions began in mid-2022 and are ongoing almost a year later. On December 10, 2022, newly released 81 70 5831 008-4 stands in York Klondyke sidings awaiting deployment. *Mark Saunders*

A modular future

RIGHT: The innovative Kirow switch and point carriers first appeared in 2014 with the delivery of 24 wagons that were coded IFA. Further batches have followed, these being a mixture of standalone vehicles and sets of inner and outer wagons. With the deck lying flat, they can be loaded with point assemblies and then tilted so that they can be transferred to yards to await installation at worksites. Unloading is carried out using special lifting beams that travel on accompanying flat wagons converted from YEA Perch. On March 7, 2023, 66421 works south at Wigan North Western with the 6X05 Carlisle Yard-Basford Hall with 37 70 9228 011-6 leading the consist. David Ratcliffe

LEFT: Built by Swedish firm Railcare, six of its RailVac machines have worked in the UK since 2012, the design evolving over time with some differences between them. These are coded KFA as they are built on the frames of former container flats with 99 70 9515 005-5 seen at Kettering on July 2, 2016, when nine months old. When in use, they are normally sandwiched in between ballast opens, one half containing fresh ballast and the other to be loaded with the old ballast sucked up by the machine. Dan Adkins

Another use of modules is for Network Rail's cable-laying train, which is normally found operating south of the Thames as and when needed. The cable drum carriers were built by Cowans Sheldon and have been mounted on EWS/DB FAA well wagons and FKA container flats over the years, depending on which could be spared. They are currently on FAAs as illustrated by 609061 at Hinksey on February 27, 2022. Rich Martin

A modular future

FEA infrastructure flats

With the rise of modular maintenance systems, container flats are increasingly seeing use on infrastructure duties, the ability to swap over their decks or put them to use on intermodal services at a future date offering the sort of flexibility that greatly appeals to wagon owners. The Greenbrier-built FEAs have led the way in this field as Simon Bendall explains.

One of Balfour Beatty's two New Track Construction machines leads the 6F27 14.36 Westbury-Crediton behind 56302 *PECO The Railway Modeller 2016 70 Years* as it departs Westbury on April 18, 2021. The two FEA wagons are at the front with the purpose-built power wagon third in line. The sleeper wagons are some of Network Rail's KRA flats originally used by Jarvis. Mark Few

Building wagons that are bespoke to a particular traffic is something that wagon owners would like to avoid where possible as it limits their potential for re-use should the designated role come to an end. Witness, for example, the vast swathes of coal hoppers that met an early demise when the bottom fell out of the power station coal market, and they proved unsuitable for aggregates use without extensive alterations.

With GB Railfreight entering the infrastructure market in the early-2000s, the company soon had need of flat wagons to support its expansion plans. However, with virtually all ex-BR types belonging to EWS, not to mention ever increasing in age, it had to turn to new builds to satisfy its needs.

As GBRf was already rapidly expanding into intermodal traffic, the idea of using a growing fleet of container flats equipped with suitable decks for engineering duties was appealing and if the work ever dried up, they could easily be transferred back to carrying shipping containers. Freightliner Heavy Haul also had need of wagons to support infrastructure work and with large numbers of new flats on the way, it too was exploring how these could be used to overcome the issue.

The most popular design at this time was the FEA spine wagon offered by Greenbrier Europe, this featuring a 60ft-long container deck with hinged spigots allowing various lengths of container to be carried. Early orders had focussed on twinsets, which were two wagons semi-permanently coupled, but a simple re-design would allow single flats

ABOVE: Freightliner FEA(E) 641023 was fitted with the short-lived 30ft track panel flat modules when recorded at Maindee West Junction, Newport, on October 31, 2006, allowing it to carry new concrete-sleepered sections. Martyn Read

ABOVE: GBRf opted to use three 20ft modules on its flats for track carrying but the result was the same as demonstrated by Metronet yellow FEA(S) 640910 at Hinksey Yard on September 22, 2016. Rich Martin

to be built with conventional drawgear at both ends, giving the flexibility needed for infrastructure work.

Freightliner singles

A total of 66 single flats, designated FEA(E), were delivered to Freightliner during 2004, 641001-066 carrying dark green and intended for both intermodal and infrastructure use. Several of the wagons were duly fitted with two 30ft flat modules each soon after delivery to allow track panels to be carried, recorded identities being 641015/21-28/30/31/33/34/39/40/42/43/59. However, their use was short-lived as soon afterwards, Freightliner lost its infrastructure renewal contracts during re-tendering, the FEAs being redeployed to maritime duties.

Also somewhat brief was the use of FEA(E) as ballast carriers, with at least 641029/3 2/34/37/41/44/47/51/53/57/58/66 each receiving two 30ft green-painted box bodies in the summer of 2005. Within three years, the boxes were noted stacked to one side at Crewe Basford Hall, but some were reunited with FEAs at the end of 2012 for several years to carry spent ballast. In this latter instance, they were mainly fitted to FEA(B) twinsets and the odd single wagon. The boxes have occasionally reappeared when required in subsequent years, but their use is typically fleeting.

GBRf orders

GB Railfreight was somewhat more committed to using FEAs on engineering jobs, it initially receiving 63 FEA(S) in 2004, 640631-93 all carrying dark blue. Some of these were again deployed to maritime or gypsum traffic but others received two types of module for infrastructure roles. Some gained three 20ft flat modules for carrying track panels and were naturally dubbed Super Salmon, while others were given three modules with dropside doors along with extension pieces over the headstocks. This created a low-sided open wagon capable of carrying 60ft rails, sleepers, and other general loads, leading to another use of the Super Tench name.

With the award of the Metronet contract, 22 additional FEA(S) were delivered in 2006, 640901-04 carrying GBRf blue while 640905-22 were new in Metronet yellow. These were again equipped with either the Salmon or Tench modules, the former featuring on about two-thirds of the batch. Following the collapse of Metronet and the conclusion of the London Underground renewal programme, this batch of flats was largely redeployed onto intermodal traffic.

Other users

Two other companies invested in small numbers of single FEAs for specific purposes. To service its slice of the London Underground renewals contract, Tube Lines subsidiary TransPlant received 13 FEA(S) wagons, 640931-43, in 2006, which were then fitted out as a Slinger rail delivery train and based at Wellingborough Yard. Like the Jarvis sets, this involved the addition of substantial lifting gantries and support structures to all wagons with 640931 and 640936 also each gaining a generator. Once the work had finished, the train went into store in 2016 for a number of years with work recently undertaken to return the wagons to traffic on intermodal duties.

Lastly, Balfour Beatty ordered six EEA(D) singles, 640571-76, and seven FEA(B) twinsets, 640501-14, in 2006. The latter along with 640573/74 became sleeper carriers while the other four single flats formed the basis of two New Track Construction (NTC) machines. This high-output tracklaying system can complete an average of 200 yards of track per hour, including laying up to 12 steel or concrete sleepers per minute. Two of the flats carry a gantry unit that moves along the train collecting the sleepers, while the other pair house a demountable truss unit that carries out the sleeper laying and threads rails into place. Power to the two trains comes from purpose-built power wagons DR78701 and DR78702.

ABOVE: GB Railfreight blue-liveried FEA(S) 640683 was carrying the Tench modules when also recorded at Hinksey Yard on December 6, 2017. These included extra extensions over the headstocks so 60ft rails could be accommodated with room to spare. Brian Daniels

ABOVE: Transplant FEA(S) 640940 shows off its extensive modifications into a Slinger wagon for delivering rail while in store at Eastleigh on April 26, 2017. The train would never work in this form again, the cranes and other deck equipment being stripped off and scrapped some five years later to allow the wagons to be reused for intermodal traffic. Brian Daniels

ABOVE: With GBRf needing more FEAs for intermodal traffic, recent years have seen the track carrying modules appear on a few Touax-owned KFA flats instead. RLS92640 demonstrates the new look at Bescot on May 1, 2021, while coupled to a Salmon. Andy Cole

A modular future

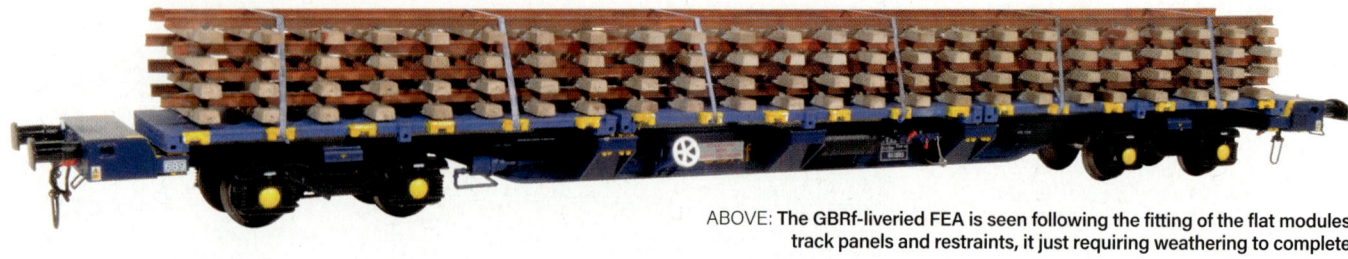

ABOVE: **The GBRf-liveried FEA is seen following the fitting of the flat modules, track panels and restraints, it just requiring weathering to complete.**

Beyond the box

Nowadays, intermodal wagons carry more than just containers. Terry Bendall describes how to build some suitable infrastructure loads using 3D printed kits for the Hattons FEA flat.

Early 2019 saw Hattons release its own-brand model of the single FEA flats in OO gauge, it was made available in several liveries including Freightliner green, GB Railfreight blue and Metronet yellow. Although the model was primarily intended for use with various intermodal containers, particularly those produced by C=Rail, a few of the wagons were supplied with track panel carrying modules.

The most useful were the two Metronet FEAs with three 20ft flats finished in dark blue while there were also two Freightliner wagons with the short-lived pair of 30ft modules. Sadly, the 20ft flat modules were not released as separate accessories which would have allowed them to be added to the GBRf liveried models if desired and other wagon types, such as Hornby's Tiphook KFA.

However, sometime later a trawl of a certain internet auction site found Resin Printed Railways offering 3D printed versions of the flat modules as well as the 30ft ballast boxes sometimes seen atop Freightliner FEAs. One set of each was ordered to see what they were like with more of the flat modules later being picked up at a show. Unfortunately, the start of this year saw the company suspend trading, at least for the moment.

Changing a flat

The prints for the track carrying flats were cleaned up as needed and then carefully marked out so holes could be drilled to accept the container locating spigots supplied with the Hattons model. Having done this, it was found that there was insufficient width to the corners of the prints to allow a hole of the necessary size to be drilled. To overcome this, some pieces of 60 thou square styrene strip were glued around the existing corners to allow the holes to be made using a 1.2mm drill bit, this giving a bit of wriggle room when getting the modules onto the wagon.

The other main job was to cut a slot at the rear of the ratchet tensioners to allow the tie down straps to be fitted. This was done using a 0.4mm drill in a mini drill to make three holes in line, which were then made into slots by carefully rocking the drill from side to side to remove the waste material. The flats were painted using Humbrol No. 25 which was a decent match for the GBRf blue. Once dry, Humbrol No. 154 was used to paint the ratchets and the modules then glued onto the FEA.

The track panel loads were made using P4 gauge Exactoscale items, with the moulded plastic sleepers painted with Humbrol No. 147 light grey and the Pandrol clips picked out with No. 27. The rails were painted with a mix of rust colours with some Railmatch sleeper grime then washed on to dull the colours. Once assembled, a further thin wash was added to tone down the sleepers and clips. The track panels were next glued in place with superglue with the tie down straps being thin slivers cut for a suitably coloured plastic bag. Six straps were added in keeping with the instructions for such a load,

Ballast in bulk

The pair of 30ft ballast boxes were found to need a lot of cleaning up since the 3D printing process left evidence of the layers of resin laid down by the printer. Some scraping and filling was done but it was difficult to get a key for the filler. A first coat of paint soon revealed a rather poor finish to the panels so to solve the problem, pieces of five thou styrene sheet were cut to fit in each panel recess to act as overlays and glued in place with superglue. Filling round the edges was fairly straightforward and a much better result was obtained.

On marking out for the spigot locating holes, it was found that these came close to the edge of the resin once again and in some cases when drilling, the holes broke through the sides. Use of filler was not very satisfactory so the corners were filed off and small triangles of 40 thou styrene glued in place and filed smooth once the glue had hardened. This gave a much better result once the holes were drilled.

The boxes were painted with Railmatch Freightliner green while for the loads, a piece of 40 thou styrene was cut to fit the inside of each box and smaller rectangles of the same material glued on top to assist in forming a hump in the load. A small piece of wood was glued under each former to fix it at an appropriate height inside the box.

The ballast load was formed by applying a layer of PVA woodworking glue and pressing the loose ballast into it and leaving it to dry. The process was repeated until an acceptable load had been created. Using PVA glue in this way allows the ballast to retain its colour. If diluted PVA or one of the ready-made ballast adhesives is used and applied with a dropper, the adhesive will take off the natural new ballast colour which is not at all desirable. The final job with both flats was to fit etched screw couplings from the Roxey Mouldings range and the supplied brake pipes.

ABOVE: **The ballast boxes make an interesting load on the Freightliner FEA, it being something of a shame that they have only seen limited use.**

A modular future

ABOVE: Using a former of styrene sheet in profiled layers gives a humped base on which the ballast can be glued. The load is also removable if need be.

ABOVE: Slices of carrier bags or masking tape make good ratchet straps in 4mm scale. The flat modules still require lettering to be added in the form of more custom transfers.

The 30ft ballast boxes were originally fitted on single Freightliner FEAs but later featured on a mix of both twin and single wagons. On December 26, 2012, FEA(E) 641059 was stabled in Sandiacre ballast sidings, Toton, loaded with spoil. *Daryl Harris-Saxton*

Modelling BR: Engineers Wagons of Privatisation

A modular future

The Lobster rebodies

Red and ribbed, Lobster is the perfect name for these DB Cargo rebuilds of predominately BDA bolster wagons, the programme putting new box bodies on old underframes. With the new Bachmann model just released, *Simon Bendall* looks at their development and two other related prototypes.

Caught reposing in the sun at Hinksey, 950603 illustrates the general look of the MXA Lobsters when still fresh from conversion on July 20, 2016. This illustrates the variant with solebar-mounted handbrake levers with its international number of 82 70 4703 030-5 positioned next to the BR number. *Brian Daniels*

The first of what would become known as Lobsters broke cover in February 2015 with the emergence of a rebuilt former BDA bogie bolster from DB Cargo's wagon works at Stoke. Still numbered 950321 but now coded MXA, the wooden floor and bolsters were completely gone to be replaced by a substantial low-height box body bolted on top of the refurbished underframe.

Finished in all over DB red apart from the bogies, but including the underframe trussing, it was the first of three prototypes used to assess the possibility of reusing the underframes of ex BR wagon types to create new bogie box wagons for aggregates, ballast, and spoil use. Stoke was to be the assembly point for these conversions using box bodies built by WH Davis at its Shirebrook workshops.

The second prototype was completed two months later in the form of MVA 910164, which was a former BBA steel wagon with its floor removed in favour of another newly fabricated, red-painted box. This was initially trialled on aggregates traffic out of Peak Forest that spring. The third of the trial rebuilds debuted in June 2015, former BAA steel wagon 900241 emerging as a MUA, its red box being somewhat shorter than its two rival designs on account of the donor underframe. It too was deployed to Peak Forest to be trialled alongside the MVA.

MXA wins out
By August 2015, it was clear that the MXA design converted from bogie bolsters had been selected for a production batch as numerous BDA and BEA wagons arrived at Stoke to be stripped down and have their underframes overhauled and repainted while awaiting their new box bodies.

The first production MXAs began to roll out of Stoke and into traffic from that November,

ABOVE: The prototype MXA, 950321, rests in Bescot Yard on August 15, 2015, six months after it first appeared. The decision to paint the underframe trussing and other fittings in red certainly resulted in a curious appearance but was not repeated on the production batch. It also did not carry an international number in this form. *Andy Cole*

96 www.keymodelworld.com

A modular future

ABOVE: The other variety of ex BDA Lobster is illustrated by 951131 or 82 70 4703 037-0, again at Hinksey on July 20, 2016. This retains the handbrake wheels on both Y25s, which were part of its conversion to air brakes in the early 1980s. Although the Lobsters were all converted at the same time and place, the positioning of the solebar lettering was not necessarily consistent between wagons. *Brian Daniels*

being largely identical to the prototype. One notable change though was the application of international 12-dgit numbers to all of the conversions as they were completed. These were displayed on the solebars alongside the existing BR six-digit numbers, which continued to be the one used to identify the wagons on TOPS. The DB red trussing given to the prototype was also not repeated, this area being black on all the production MXAs.

By the beginning of 2016, a total of around 200 Lobster conversions was envisaged by DB. However, as some BDA/BEA underframes were prepared, it was found they were too fatigued to be re-used and were rejected from the programme. To give sufficient chassis, a number of the closely related BMA aluminium ingot carriers had also been added to the donor list and the first of these emerged as an MXA that January. Originally built as Boplates, they retained their numbers in the 965xxx series in addition to their assigned international identities.

The planned Lobster conversions were finally concluded in August 2016 with the departure of 951065, this bringing the total to 210. However, this was not the end of the project as a number of the rebuilt wagons were soon returned to Stoke following structural issues with the reconditioned underframes, this particularly affecting the former BMAs. Rather than conduct expensive repairs, the solution was to remove the body and transfer it onto another prepared underframe, the old one going for scrap. Around a dozen bodies were remounted in this manner, one of the beneficiaries being the prototype MXA 950321 which had been stored at Stoke for some time. This received a production body and was returned to traffic.

Since their introduction, the Lobsters have once again seen use in ballast and spoil traffic as well as carrying recovered sleepers for recycling, with their appearance having an impact on the various out of favour Coalfish designs. Initially at least, the MXAs tended to be formed on their own in trains of varying lengths but over time have become a bit more mixed with other types, again seeing use across the country.

ABOVE: Less than 20 BMAs were included in the Lobster rebodying programme, and this number dropped even further when several of the underframes developed faults and the boxes were transferred onto new donors. 965050, or 82 70 4703 089-1, is one of those that did survive and was recorded at Kingsthorpe on May 8, 2016. *Dan Adkins*

Bachmann boils the pot

With the Lobsters being converted mostly from BDAs, enterprising modellers seeking to produce them initially turned to stripping down the Bachmann model of the bogie bolsters and adding a new body, be it scratchbuilt from styrene or resin cast. The Cambrian kit of the BDAs could also be used for the same purpose. However, early 2023 saw Bachmann announce a RTR version of the MXAs in OO gauge which has newly arrived with retailers.

Rather than just repurpose its old BDA, Bachmann has started again for the Lobsters with a new chassis that includes full brake equipment detail and the open framework that is visible underneath the ballast box. The manufacturer has also tooled both types of handbrake with one

release featuring the solebar-mounted brake levers and the other the handbrake discs on the Y25 bogies. The box is also nicely moulded with the whole model looking striking in its DB red.

Modelling BR: Engineers Wagons of Privatisation 97

A modular future

LEFT: Of the other two prototype rebodies, former BBA, now MVA, 910164 was not used in infrastructure traffic but is worth illustrating for completeness. It is pictured at Peak Forest on October 18, 2015, six months after it was completed and deployed on aggregates services. Although it remained a one off, it was useful and continued in traffic until 2019. Since then, it has been stored in Acton Yard. *John Dedman*

RIGHT: Also recorded at Peak Forest on October 18, 2015, was MUA 900241, four months after its release from Stoke. As the shortest of the three, this restricted its payload and its time on aggregates traffic was short-lived. September 2017 saw it briefly reported in infrastructure services working between Eastleigh and Hoo Junction but since then it has been out of traffic at the Kent yard. *John Dedman*

The Lobsters certainly brightened up infrastructure services following their introduction as illustrated at Rearsby on January 7, 2018, as 15 MXAs form the leading portion of the 6B10 12.00 Luffenham-Toton working. Powered by 66112, the consist includes the prototype 950321 fifth in formation, its red trussing clearly standing out. On the rear are a number of MHA Coalfish and a solitary mesh-sided OBA. *Paul Biggs*

The World's Fastest Growing Aviation Website

Join us online

SUBSCRIBE TODAY!

"In-depth content and high-quality photography"
Stew

"Well worth the money"
Andy

"A great place for aviation geeks!"
Kenneth

GREAT REASONS TO SUBSCRIBE

- In-depth articles, videos, quizzes and more, with new material added daily

- From historic and military aviation to commercial and simulation – *Key.Aero* has it all

- Exclusive interactive content you won't find anywhere else

- A fully searchable archive

- Access to all the leading aviation magazines

- Membership to an engaged, global aviation community

- Access on any device – anywhere, anytime

www.key.aero

Subscribe FROM JUST £5.99 for unlimited access

A modular future

Although coded MLA, the Wascosa wagons have a number of differences from the previous batches, particularly the solebar design, which is more like the earlier JNA Falcons. There are also no inspection steps or doors. A brand new 81 70 5932 204-7 stands in Hinksey Yard on August 17, 2022, between two of its predecessors. *Brian Daniels*

The Wascosa fleet

For its most recent wagons, Network Rail has returned to leasing, partnering with Wascosa and GB Railfreight to introduce further box wagons and also module-fitted flats to finally see off the Salmons. Simon Bendall **looks at the latest yellow additions.**

Network Rail announced one of its largest wagon orders for some years in October 2020 as it unveiled an agreement with Swiss-based wagon leasing firm Wascosa to introduce 570 new wagons for infrastructure use. The deal was a significant expansion for Wascosa as, although well known on the continent, it had not supplied wagons to the UK before.

Slightly disappointingly, it did not herald the arrival of the company's bold blue and orange livery in this country, yellow being the order of the day, but the two types of box wagon were certainly branded to be noticed. Also involved in the ten-year deal was GB Railfreight, which would cover the maintenance side of things, while Greenbrier Europe was selected as the manufacturer using its existing and already approved designs.

First to arrive in November and December 2021 were 50 JNA high-sided boxes to supplement the IOAs on virtual quarry duties, these being numbered 81 70 5932 151 to 200. These are all but identical to the numerous JNAs now deployed on aggregate services across the country and were soon in use. During their 16 months in traffic to date, they have been noted operating as both block formations and mixed in with their predecessors, helping to release the bulk ballast restricted MRAs for rebuilding.

Next to appear from December 2021 were the first of 260 additional MLA low-sided ballast opens, which once again were for

ABOVE: One of GBRf's converted European-specification Class 66s, 66795 *Bescot LDC*, traverses Worting Junction on July 8, 2022, with the 6M26 Eastleigh-Mountsorrel empties. This was formed of 16 Wascosa JNAs that were already starting to get covered in ballast dust. *Stephen Stubbs*

A modular future

ABOVE: **The unique 'eco' livery carried by 68006** *Pride of the North* **is certainly eye catching as demonstrated on April 20, 2023, as the DRS machine powers through Low Gill with the 6K06 Shap to Basford Hall loaded ballast. This is again making good use of the Wascosa JNAs with 15 examples in tow.** Mark Latham

possession work and to hasten the demise of the MHA/MPA Coalfish and the remaining MFAs and MTAs. Numbered 81 70 5932 201 to 460, deliveries to the UK were completed in January 2023 and they have become an increasingly common sight across much of the country mixed in with similar 'gondola' ballast wagon types.

Salmon replacements

The most interesting part of the announcement was the fleet of 260 flat wagons, which turned out to be a further batch of FEA container wagons, these all being 'singles' with drawgear at both ends. Deliveries commenced in February 2022 with all of 81 70 4521 001-260 in the country 11 months later. These flats were to be paired with a number of modules developed by GBRf and were again based around 20ft ISO spacings. These turned out to be further builds of the Salmon flatbeds and Tench cages with a new bolster and stanchion variant based on the Mullet.

While some of the FEAs arrived through the Channel Tunnel with the modules already fitted, others arrived empty to be equipped here. While this programme was put in place, GBRf used a number of the module-less flats on its intermodal services for a time, running them in. After a somewhat protracted commissioning, the fleet was beginning to appear regularly in traffic in the spring of 2023, particularly carrying track panels and new sleepers.

Once their deployment is completed, this should allow withdrawals of the elderly Salmons to commence at long last while the remaining YLA Mullets are also likely to be in the firing line as their underframes are just as old.

ABOVE: **The Wascosa lettering given to the two types of box wagons is certainly bold and rather contrasts with the small Network Rail logos. JNA 81 70 5932 181-7 rolls through Kennington, to the north of Oxford, on February 18, 2022, on its way back to Leicestershire for more ballast.** Brian Daniels

Wascosa from Revolution

Revolution Trains is so far the only manufacturer to produce the Wascosa fleet in miniature as it already had the JNA box wagon tooling available, it just needed a few tweaks to take account of altered details. The Wascosa bulk ballast JNAs have therefore already been released in N gauge with the model of 81 70 5932 172-6 pictured here, while the same process is now underway in OO gauge after the livery was announced last November, although a release date has yet to be set.

Modelling BR: Engineers Wagons of Privatisation 101

A modular future

RIGHT: Based on observations, the Salmon flat modules are by far the dominant type fitted to the FEAs, which is no surprise as transporting track panels and sleepers requires a sizeable fleet. As with the earlier FEAs, these are made up of sets of three based on 20ft ISO standards with ratchet tensioners down the sides. 81 70 4524 066-7 is seen in Bescot Yard soon after delivery on July 17, 2022. Andy Cole

LEFT: In contrast, a straw poll would suggest the Mullet modules will be the least common, these aping the bolsters and stanchions of their YLA namesakes in order to carry rail lengths. Ten bolsters are provided alongside the ratchet tensioners with loaded examples noted in traffic during April 2023. Space constraints mean the Wascosa lettering is more restrained on the FEAs with 81 70 4524 064-2 recorded at Bescot on the same day. Andy Cole

RIGHT: Completing the module options seen to date on the FEAs is the Tench, which largely mirrors the design seen on earlier FEAs once again but with mesh rather than sheet metal for the side panels. The Network Rail logo also adorns the wagon's spine with the handbrake wheel passing through the large number panel. 81 70 4524 070-9 was also soaking up the sun at Bescot on July 17, 2022. Andy Cole

A modular future

6K05 – a train of variety

The weekday infrastructure workings that support Network Rail's National Delivery Service vary considerably in both length and composition. To illustrate the range of wagons that can be paired together, **David Ratcliffe** focuses on the service that runs between Carlisle and Crewe, which is often routed via the scenic Settle & Carlisle line and also features an array of DRS traction.

Following many years of declining freight traffic, which in 1984 had led to the threat of its complete closure, the Settle & Carlisle line began to slowly recover during the second half of that decade as much needed repairs were made to the route's infrastructure. Consequently, the line was again host to a number of Anglo-Scottish coal workings during the 1990s while 6C02, the morning northbound infrastructure train from Crewe Basford Hall to Carlisle Kingmoor Yard, would occasionally be routed via Blackburn and the S&C.

By 2006, 6C02 invariably ran directly north over the WCML via Tebay as did its southbound equivalent 6K05, which was then timed as the 13.28 departure from Carlisle to Crewe. This changed during 2011 when 6K05 was rescheduled to depart from Kingmoor around an hour earlier and run south via Ribblehead. Not only did this bring extra freight to the route, which by now was also seeing block trains of cement, gypsum, and timber, it was a most welcome addition to the S&C as infrastructure services are among the most varied and interesting mixed freights to be seen.

Since the summer of 2013, Direct Rail Services has provided the haulage for 6K05 with the train usually powered by one of its Class 66s. However, Class 37s and Class 68s, either singly or in pairs, as well as Class 57s can sometimes turn up on the working. Once in a while, the train still runs south via Tebay, especially when a Class 88 is provided as motive power, while it is not unusual to see locos from other freight operators in the consist. This is typically one or more Freightliner Class 66s being hauled back to Basford Hall after use on weekend engineering work north of the border.

A mix of types

As illustrated and detailed in the sample table of consists, a plethora of different engineering wagon types can find their way into 6K05. Unsurprisingly, low-sided open ballast/spoil box wagons, such as JNA Falcon, MHA and MLA, are among the most common. The service is also used to move a steady supply of new sleepers from the vast stockpile that Network Rail keeps at Carlisle Kingmoor. Both YWA Salmon and module-fitted Tiphook and Railease KFA bogie flat wagons have handled this traffic, while since early 2023 the new Wascosa FEA Salmons have also begun to appear on this flow. Another common type in recent years has been the YKA Ospreys, which are former Salmons modified to carry track panels. Much redundant timber-sleeper track is dispatched from across the country to Basford Hall for

ABOVE: With TransPennine Express continuing to underuse its Mk.5 sets, the matching Class 68s are no strangers to appearing on DRS freight workings, be it nuclear flasks or infrastructure duties. On June 24, 2020, 68032 *Courageous* is recorded amid the splendour of Ais Gill as it heads the 6K05 12.46 Carlisle Yard-Basford Hall. On this occasion, the train was formed of MHA/MPA Coalfish of both body types, with at least some of the wagons loaded with scrap rail cut into short lengths. Dave McAlone

processing in the materials recovery site established in part of the yard.

On-going track renewals in Cumbria, southwest Scotland and the Glasgow area also occasionally results in the impressive Kirow-built IFA modular tilting wagons, otherwise known as 'Tilt-Beds', appearing in the Carlisle to Crewe workings. These are used to carry switch and crossing assemblies, and are working back to the Progress Rail site at Beeston Yard, near Nottingham. When these IFAs are included, the train's reporting number is changed to 6X05, reflecting the fact that even when tilted in the diagonal travelling position, the lower edge of the 'Tilt-Bed' is still out of gauge. Consequently, the wagons require a RT3973 form for all movements and must only be signalled over the designated lines.

Modelling BR: Engineers Wagons of Privatisation **103**

A modular future

A selection of 6K05 consists

Date	Loco	Wagons
14/06/17	66423	5 MHA (spoil), JNA (ballast), 5 MHA (spoil), 6 MTA, SPA, 6 MTA, SPA, 3 MTA
06/06/18	68004	MHA (ballast), 5 OCA, FJA
06/06/19	66422	2 MLA, 4 JNA, MLA, IEA, 5 JNA
01/07/19	66429	2 YLA, 3 YKA (all loaded with track panels), 3 OCA, 7 YKA (track panels)
30/07/20	66303/66427	5 MRA, 2 Tiphook KFA (new sleepers), 3 YWA (new sleepers), OCA, JNA, MLA, 6 JNA, MLA
10/08/20	66091/66508/66598	3 YWA (track panels), 2 Tiphook KFA, 6 YWA (all loaded with sections of old track)
21/09/20	66108	5 JJA, 5 HQA
26/04/21	68002	3 YKA (track panels), 12 YXA/IFA (all loaded with old concrete sleepers)
02/06/21	66429	4 IFA Tilt-Bed, YRA, 3 IFA Tilt-Bed, OCA, Tiphook KFA (lifting beam), SB Rail 25-tonne crane, YWA
20/07/21	66301/66176	10 MXA, 12 MHA/MPA (all loaded with old concrete sleepers)
22/09/21	66305	2 JNA, 6 YWA (new sleepers), 6 JNA
06/10/21	68016	2 MLA, 3 JNA
17/08/22	66433/66434	2 JNA, 7 MXA (two loaded with new ballast, the rest empty)
20/01/23	57304	MXA, JNA
23/02/23	88006/66413	IFA, YSA (HOBC support wagons), 4 MLA, JNA, 4 YWA (new sleepers), 2 FEA (new sleepers), 8 JNA

LEFT: The DRS-liveried Class 68s are frequently used on 6K05 as illustrated by 68002 *Intrepid* as it arrives at Hellifield on April 26, 2021. On this day, the consist was three YKA Osprey loaded with track panels and a dozen YXA carrying concrete sleepers for recycling. David Ratcliffe

RIGHT: Frequently, old concrete sleepers for disposal or recycling are conveyed in low-sided box wagon types such as MHA Coalfish and MXA Lobsters. Occasionally, something more unusual can appear in 6K05, such as YXA DR92651, as seen at Hellifield on June 1, 2021. This was one of 65 YXA bogie flats built by WH Davis in 2004, which were numbered in the on-track plant series as DR92601-65 and initially used to carry new sleepers for the Matisa Track Renewals Train. When new, all of the individual cradles were painted white but this led to sighting difficulties during their unloading, so they were repainted in a number of different pastel shades. A further 50 wagons to a largely identical design followed in 2009, these being coded IFA and numbered 31 70 4629 001-50. David Ratcliffe

LEFT: During 2020, a small number of former Railease and Tiphook KFA bogie container flats were leased by Network Rail and fitted with flat modules of the same style used on selected FEAs. In this form, they are used to carry both new sleepers and old track. Loaded with two lengths of timber-sleepered track, TIPH93466 is pictured at Hellifield on August 10 that year. Hornby produces this type of KFA in 4mm scale while Revolution Trains has done the same in 2mm, albeit in both cases without the flat modules. David Ratcliffe

A modular future

ABOVE: In the simplified DRS blue livery, 66426 heads 6K05 at Ribblehead on April 23, 2018, with an OCA open leading the formation followed by two 105-tonne Kirow KRC250UK diesel hydraulic cranes and their attendant beam carriers and Salmon match wagons. Both cranes are in the colours of Swietelsky Babcock Rail (SB Rail) and from the DRK81623-25 series, while the two KFA beam carrier wagons from the FS97413-15 range were also purpose built for the role by Trinity Rail. With a lifting capacity of 25-tonnes, these Kirows are used to recover life-expired track panels or handle switch and crossing components, as well as remove and replace signal gantries and other lineside equipment. *Trevor Mann*

RIGHT: Now under DRS control, former Fastline machine 66305 rounds the curve into Hellifield station on April 8, 2019, with Freightliner's 66957 *Stephenson Locomotive Society 1909-2009* dead in tow. The latter Class 66 was being returned to Crewe after weekend engineering work in Scotland as were the ten empty low-sided box wagons. These consist of seven JNA Falcons sandwiching a pair of MLAs in different liveries. *David Ratcliffe*

LEFT: During 2019, DRS agreed a deal with DB Cargo for the long-term lease of five otherwise surplus Class 66s and these were soon a common sight heading 6K05 over the S&C. Having just crossed the famous 440 yard long Ribblehead Viaduct, 66108 heads south on April 15, 2021, the loco being dispatched to Toton later that month for repainting in DRS blue. The flat wagons are all loaded with new sleepers and are a mix of YWA Salmons and module-fitted KFAs. *David Ratcliffe*

Modelling BR: Engineers Wagons of Privatisation **105**

A modular future

LEFT: On occasions, 6K05 can feature one or more of DRS' diminishing Class 37 fleet, an event that is guaranteed to get photographers out. On June 16, 2021, Regional Railways-liveried 37425 *Sir Robert McAlpine/ Concrete Bob* leads equally retro-liveried 37402 *Stephen Middlemore* through Appleby and past the restored water tower with a short 6K05. On this occasion, it was formed of four MXA Lobsters and three YWA Salmons loaded with new sleepers. Dave McAlone

RIGHT: Double-headed Class 68s are less common on 6K05 but on September 28, 2018, 68034 was leading ScotRail-liveried 68006 *Daring* on 6K05 as they cross Ais Gil Viaduct. This time around the working featured YDA Octopus wagons from one of Network Rail's high-output ballast cleaning trains while the leading vehicle is a YSA workshop and conveyor support wagon built by WH Davis in 2004 and numbered in the DR92701-06 series. Dave McAlone

On a fine February 27, 2019, 66302 slogs towards Shotlock Hill Tunnel on the S&C with 6K05, it conveying 15 HQA autoballasters on this day. As ever, the hoppers are formed in sets of five with the first and last now discoloured to brown from their initial yellow livery while the middle set retains the original beige and blue livery but suitably rebranded. Sandy Biggs

A modular future

ABOVE: With Wild Boar Fell forming the backdrop, 57304 *Pride of Cheshire* was not exactly taxed as it powers a featherweight 6K05 at Ais Gill on January 20, 2023, this featuring a MXA Lobster and JNA Falcon. Such light loads can occasionally be seen on the trunk infrastructure workings across the country and while some may question their viability in isolation, the loco is working a set diagram and will typically have more meaningful work at some point during the day. Sandy Biggs

ABOVE: When 6K05 is worked by a Class 88 hybrid, the train is typically sent via the West Coast Main Line to avoid over-burdening the small diesel engine. However, on March 25, 2022, the partnering of 88007 *Electra* in multiple with 68005 *Defiant* allowed the usual S&C route to be taken. Recorded at Hellifield Green, the leading three wagons make up one of Balfour Beatty's two New Track Construction (NTC) machines and these are followed by a set of five empty MCA/MDA ballast opens and ten YWA Salmon loaded with new concrete sleepers. Mark Latham

The inclusion of IFA tilting-deck point carriers in the formation of the Carlisle to Crewe working on July 2, 2019, meant the train was running under the revised reporting code of 6X05 as 66429 leads Chiltern silver 68015 through Jack Green, near Preston. The working also features six YKA Osprey loaded with track panels, a mesh-sided OBA open and two YRA support wagons, which carry the lifting beams required to unload the switch and crossing assemblies. Mark Latham

The war on leaves

Network Rail's fleet of Railhead Treatment Trains will notch up 20 years of operation this autumn, the use of the seasonal watercannon and sandite sets having been expanded and refined since introduced in their original form back in 2003. Simon Bendall **looks at their history over the past two decades.**

ABOVE: Nothing defined the annual Railhead Treatment Train season more than the sight of a pair of Direct Rail Services Class 20/3s pottering around the countryside with their accompanying FEA wagons jetting away. Such was the case on November 23, 2006, as 20307 and 20313 top and tail the 1Z61 08.45 Stowmarket-Norwich at Roudham, near Thetford. The RHTT set is a combined sandite and water jetting formation. Gareth Bayer

As this century began, Railtrack had an array of rolling stock at its disposal to combat the annual problem of autumn leaf fall. While the issue had become a running joke with the media and public, the build-up of compacted and hardened leaf mulch on railheads during the season had only become worse in the preceding decade as lineside vegetation was allowed to grow out of control.

These slippery conditions were a particular problem for the ever increasing number of comparatively lightweight and disc-braked multiple units, which could lock their wheels under braking and slide through station platforms or, more seriously, red signals and level crossings. Apart from the safety implications, locked wheelsets would suffer from flat spots, which at their worse would see a train taken out of service until remedied.

At this time, the main weapon to deal with low adhesion was to apply sandite to the rails where required, this being a sticky sand-based paste. During the 1980s and early 1990s, British Rail had converted a number of redundant multiple units and a few loco-hauled vehicles for the purpose of sandite application.

However, by 2000, these were increasingly life expired with spare parts becoming an issue, while the retention of driver knowledge was also a problem as their passenger-carrying equivalents were withdrawn.

Some experiments with high pressure water jetting had taken place with Railtrack having three former Mk.1 Motorail GUVs in use as water cannons. Numbered LNE99025-27, these were typically found operating in the northwest, northeast and east of England and were paired with blue-painted TTA water tankers hired from EG Steele. Motive power was provided by EWS, typically in the form of top and tail Class 37s or sometimes Class 31s.

The second half of the 1990s had also seen a number of Class 37s equipped to lay sandite with the storage container being fitted in the former boiler compartment. Application equipment was added to the bogie sideframes while a tell-tale external filling point was inserted into one bodyside.

Enter the MPVs

The late 1990s saw Railtrack make its first move towards modernising its seasonal fleet with an order for 25 Multi-Purpose Vehicles (MPVs) from German manufacturer Windhoff. Consisting of a powered master unit and unpowered slave, the two-car sets were designed to be capable of a range of roles, including sandite and de-icer application, water jetting and weedkilling, by swapping around the on-board modules. The first two MPVs, DR98901/51 and DR98902/52, were delivered in 1998 for trials with the remainder, DR98903/53 to DR98925/75, following in 1999 and 2000. However, their introduction to service was a protracted affair with a number of teething problems needing to be overcome.

A further seven sets, DR98926/76 to DR98932/82, followed in 2001, these featuring a number of upgrades such as a powered slave vehicle and modified suspension to allow 75mph operation. This batch was intended specifically for the erstwhile Southern Region but today a large number of MPVs from the first build can also be found based in the southeast.

Elsewhere in the UK, MPVs have become particularly concentrated in the northwest, covering the Merseyrail network and

The war on leaves

surrounding area from their base at Wigan Springs Branch, as well as Slateford, near Edinburgh, from where they tackle suburban lines around the Scottish capital and Glasgow.

Loco-hauled solution

The autumn of 2003 brought the first use of loco-hauled wagon sets, these being termed Railhead Treatment Trains or RHTTs by Network Rail as they could combine water cannon and sandite application if required. However, these were not formed of the now familiar FEA wagons but instead utilised 60ft KFA container flats built by Rautaruukki of Finland in 1987/88. Originally owned by Tiphook and then GE Rail Services, they were some of the first wagons to be acquired by Network Rail following its creation in 2002.

Accompanying the KFAs was the first appearance of the blue-painted generator/jetting modules and the associated water tanks, these sharing design traits with those used on the MPVs. This new equipment was deployed in two forms with some KFAs just carrying three water tanks for use with the trio of aforementioned Mk.1 GUV water cannon vans, the flats replacing the previously used TTAs. These formations largely operated from Healy Mills during the 2003 season, top and tailed by EWS Class 37s.

The same traction could also be found powering pairs of KFAs in the now familiar manner with one wagon featuring a generator/jetting module and two water tanks while the other carried additional tanks. Such formations were recorded operating from locations such as Peterborough and Didcot as well as along the North Wales coast. In some instances though, the KFA carrying the extra water tanks could be omitted, leaving the locos to just work the single jetting wagon.

The KFAs returned once again for the 2004 leaf fall campaign but many other changes were evident. Most noticeable was an increase in the number of RHTTs deployed with a total of 20 loco-hauled formations created. Also still in use were two of the Class 37s fitted with sandite equipment in the form of 37670 and 37676 but the water cannon GUVs did not reappear for the season, having been ousted by the superior capabilities of the wagon sets.

The motive power for 2004 also saw changes as with the EWS Class 37 fleet now in decline, Class 66s and Class 67s were deployed to help out. While there were still around 30 Type 3s available for the work, the '66s' were utilised on East Anglia routes while the '67s' could be found working off Doncaster and Didcot. Other freight operators were also drafted in for the first time on a limited basis, with GB Railfreight deploying a few Peterborough-based Class 66/7s and Direct Rail Services supplying Class 37s, the latter notably covering the Settle and Carlisle line.

New wagons

The summer of 2005 saw Network Rail receive a new fleet of 50 FEA-F wagons for use on RHTT duties, these having been built by Greenbrier Europe in Poland. These replaced the KFAs on all RHTT workings that autumn with the various modules being transferred across and extras added given the increased size of the fleet. Remaining in use today, the FEAs are numbered 642001-050 and are single wagons with drawgear at each end and capable of carrying three 20ft modules.

A feature of the FEA-F variant is the presence of jumper cable connections on the bufferbeams as the wagons are through-wired to allow locos fitted with either Blue Star or AAR multiple working equipment to communicate while running in top and tail formation. Both the water jetting and sandite application are activated via remote control with the operator located in the leading locomotive cab. Neither process is continuous, with known low-adhesion areas instead being targeted along with any other trouble spots reported by traincrew, the latter being something that can change from week to week.

The make-up of the RHTTs also varies by route with two-wagon sets configured for either water jetting only or for both jetting and sandite application. In the former case, the FEAs will carry a generator/jetting module and five tanks while a combined function formation will see two of the water tanks sacrificed for two sandite modules.

As some routes cover considerable distances, a third FEA can be added to a set, this carrying three additional tanks to give sufficient water for the diagram. Normally, this additional wagon has gone in the middle of the set but on the northwest circuit from Kingmoor, it typically goes at one end with the jetting wagon moved into the centre of the formation.

Also of note is that the generator/jetting modules feature two different power unit types, the original build have a 12-litre engine while later versions have a smaller nine-litre design. This is one of the reasons why the same FEAs and modules are typically deployed to the same operating bases every year as it ensures the local maintenance crews are totally familiar with the sets and any modifications they may have made themselves.

A standard two-wagon water-cannon RHTT with five tank modules can carry some 85,500 litres of water. This is fired at a pressure of up to 1,500 bar out of the water cannon nozzles mounted beneath one of the wagons onto the rails to clean away the leave mulch. So intense is the pressure that the water will soon cut into the railheads if the jets are left on while the train is stationary! The usual train speed for jetting is 60mph but this can be decreased to 20mph for heavily contaminated lines while sandite can be laid at up to 40mph.

Since the FEAs were introduced in 2005, all five of the principal freight operators have been involved in RHTT operations to some degree or another with EWS/DB, Direct Rail Services and GB Railfreight being the most prolific while Freightliner and Colas have been rather more sporadic in taking on the work. During this time, the various companies have deployed an array of motive power, both from their own fleets and, on occasions, hired from elsewhere.

Maintenance & deployment

During the autumn, the RHTT sets are generally maintained at their various operating bases across the country. One exception is Stowmarket, which is such a cramped site that exams and other repairs are undertaken at Dereham on the Mid Norfolk Railway with sets making daily trips to and from the preserved line. Given that RHTTs are continuously operating in poor railhead conditions as they pass over their own water, slipping and consequently wheelflats are a regular occurrence with sets needing to visit wheel lathes on numerous occasions as the season progresses.

ABOVE: Clearly displaying the origins of the RHTT concept, 37712 tails the 6T78 Carlisle-Nunthorpe water cannon through Tees Yard on October 30, 2003, with Loadhaul-liveried 37516 leading. In tow is one of the three converted Mk.1 GUVs, these having originally carried the orangey-brown, white, and grey Railtrack livery before receiving the more attractive lime green and dark blue shown here. Providing the water supply is one of the newly acquired KFA flats loaded with 20ft tank modules.
Simon Bendall Collection

Modelling BR: Engineers Wagons of Privatisation **109**

The war on leaves

ABOVE: One half of a sandite/water jetting RHTT set is illustrated at Norwich on September 22, 2005, in the form of brand new FEA-F 642003. This features a water tank to the left and a sandite module to the right with the jetting and generator unit in between. Following the light brown hose on the underframe shows the location of the water spray nozzle by the inner bogie, while the sandite discharge pipe is at the outer end by the other bogie. *Gareth Bayer*

Outside of the autumn, all of the RHTTs are maintained by Network Rail at the former York Works. Although only used for three months each year, the huge mileages accumulated in this time take a considerable toll with all of the wagons and modules needing extensive servicing to prepare them for the next campaign.

During August and September each year, the RHTT sets are distributed across the country to their operating bases. The manner in which this is achieved varies with both DRS and GBRf typically collecting a long string of wagons for direct movement. While DB can also undertake direct transfers, it additionally makes use of scheduled freight trains to move some RHTT sets part of the way, giving rise to some unlikely wagon combinations. The motive power for these moves can also be interesting, featuring loco classes that are not normally involved with the autumn operations, such as Class 60s. Once the leaf fall campaign is over, typically in early to mid December, the filthy wagons are returned to York by a similar combination of methods, although it can be January or occasionally later before all of the sets make it back home.

EWS/DB operations

In its various incarnations, EWS and now DB has carried out RHTT operations every year since they commenced in 2003. The company's contribution has perhaps been rather overlooked throughout this time though as once Class 37s ceased to be employed after 2004, the deployment of Class 66s and Class 67s has generally failed to maintain the interest of enthusiasts. The company has also tended to cover many of the less interesting and photogenic routes in the middle of the country.

For 2006, the RHTT areas assigned to EWS included Westbury, Salisbury, Newbury and Reading from sets based at Bristol Barton Hill, Teesside, and the Tyne Valley from Carlisle Upperby, the Cardiff Valleys from East Usk and south and west Wales from Margam. Other RHTT bases were Peterborough for the east of England, St Blazey for Devon and Cornwall, Wigan Springs Branch where two circuits covered Greater Manchester and Merseyside, Temple Mills in East London with workings over the c2c network and around North London and finally from Didcot, where sets covered Swindon and the Malverns along with Oxford, Southall and Basingstoke. All were booked for Class 66s except for Barton Hill, where Class 67s were provided.

For the 2007 season, the track machine sidings at Broxbourne replaced the now closed Temple Mills depot as the base for the east and north London RHTTs while duties operated both north and south from Peterborough after EWS took over the Great Northern workings from GBRf, with Class 67s seeing much employment on the ECML. A new RHTT working was also introduced over the Midland Main Line, this being a regular turn for the Spanish-built GMs. The latter working was in the news again during 2008/09 after EWS deployed the executive train duo of 67029 and Mk.3b DVT 82146 to work either end of the two FEA wagons, although when unavailable, the DVT's place was taken by another Class 67.

DB alterations

Prior to the 2009 season, many of the RHTT contracts were re-tendered by Network Rail, this resulting in the now rebranded DB Schenker taking on the bulk of the work. Colas was ousted from the West Country with St Blazey restored as the operating base while DRS lost the London end duties on both the Great Western and West Coast routes, DB opting to use Didcot and Bescot as the respective servicing locations. The 'blue team' also surrendered the North Wales and Yorkshire circuits as well as the Highlands diagram from Inverness. A single Class 66 was typically deployed on the Holyhead working and a solitary Class 67 was entrusted with the Scottish working while both General Motors types shared the Yorkshire workload. Notably, DB had to request dispensation from Network Rail to use the heavy Class 67s on the weight restricted lines around West Yorkshire, having dropped its initial plans to reinstate Class 37s. While this was agreed to, the RHTT set had to shed three water tanks to bring the weight down.

For 2010, the major change for DB was motive power related with around a dozen of the Class 66s modified for use with Euro Cargo Rail (ECR) being returned from France, many finding their way onto RHTTs. With many more Sheds available, the Class 67s were largely not needed, only the Inverness diagram largely sticking with

ABOVE: For many parts of the UK, this has been the typical look of the annual RHTT operation for some 18 years - a pair of EWS-liveried Class 66s top and tailing two FEA flats. Only in more recent years has the once all-prevailing EWS maroon begun to give way to DB red as repaints continue. Pictured on October 4, 2005, 66104 leads 66153 off Peterborough shed following servicing ready for another jetting and sandite-laying session on the GE/GN 'Joint Line'. *Gareth Bayer*

The war on leaves

a Spanish-built GM. The Midland Main Line duty was turned over to 'Eurosheds' while standard '66/0s' covered the Yorkshire duties, again with eventual Network Rail approval.

One new route for DB Class 66s was over the Metropolitan Line between Amersham and Harrow-on-the-Hill as part of a revised Chiltern Line working, for which 66001/17/19 were fitted with the tripcock equipment required to operate the London Underground signalling system. Initially supplementing Chiltern Railways' converted Class 117 water cannon set 960301, the loco-hauled working eventually displaced the ageing DMU with the three modified Class 66s the only ones to be seen on the duty through to the end of the 2017 season.

The South Yorkshire and Lincolnshire RHTTs became a magnet for photographers for 2011 following Network Rail's decision not to allow the use of Class 66s or Class 67s over the weight restricted routes this time around. DB Schenker was therefore forced to hire six Class 20s to fulfil its obligations with BR blue 20096 and Railfreight triple grey 20901 and 20905 coming from HNRC while the Class 20 Locomotive Society supplied Railfreight Red Stripe 20227. Completing the line-up were Michael Owen's BR green 20189 and BR blue 20142.

Across the country, change was also evident on the Crewe-based circuit covering mid and north Wales as with ETCS cab signalling now active on the Cambrian line, only Network Rail's yellow-painted Class 97/3s could be deployed on the RHTT working to Machynlleth. The locos undertook the whole diagram as a result, which also visited Holyhead. Among the other DB Schenker RHTT workings, the number of ECR Class 66s available for 2011 was much reduced, these seeing use on the West Anglia and c2c routes in particular. As a result, Class 67s returned to the Great Western, Great Northern and Midland Main Line circuits, the latter again employing the silver Mk.3b DVT from the management train most of the time.

For 2012, Class 67 involvement was restricted to just the Inverness diagram as ECR Class 66s were deployed on the Toton-West Hampstead working with standard DB Sheds used from Didcot. The Class 97/3s remained in charge on the North Wales circuit with some assistance from hired-in DRS Class 37/4s on occasions when working away from the Cambrian line. There was little change between 2013-17 across the DB duties, although the Midland diagram alternated between pairs of Class 66s and assorted colourful Class 67s, or sometimes one of each. Additionally, '67s' were again found on the Didcot circuits in 2015 but otherwise it was Sheds across the board.

The autumn of 2018 saw DB's slice of the RHTT pie shrink as the Chiltern duty was taken over by Freightliner while Colas claimed the Midland Main Line and East Midlands for a time along with Bristol workings. DB still held a number of key duties though, including Bescot for the West Coast Main Line and Peterborough for the East Coast and east of England. Adding to this were the Margam, Didcot and St Blazey circuits, not to mention Inverness.

In subsequent years, the DB circuits have ebbed and flowed, for example DRS would

ABOVE: Two of DRS' retro-liveried Class 37/4s were in charge of the 3Z14 Cleethorpes-Bridlington RHTT as they pass New Barnetby on November 14, 2020, not that the colours are particularly discernible beneath the all-over coat of grot that soon accumulates during high-pressure jetting. Leading the way is BR large logo blue 37402 *Stephen Middlemore* with 37419 *Carl Haviland* in its InterCity Mainline scheme on the rear. The presence of five water tanks alongside the generator module marks this out as a water jetting-only formation. *Mark Latham*

retake the Inverness operation from 2019 and GB Railfreight the West Coast Main Line 12 months later. However, new areas have opened up, most notably across the Central Belt of Scotland where Class 67-hauled RHTTs were introduced from 2020. Operating from Slateford, these were brought in to work alongside the MPVs to improve the frequency with which lines were treated.

DRS operations

Having become involved in RHTT workings from 2004, DRS took on further routes the following year, including the Cambrian line (then still signalled using RETB radio equipment) and around North Wales. East Anglia workings from a new operating base at Stowmarket also commenced while the Settle & Carlisle circuit was retained. As well as Class 37s, the Class 20/3s began their association with RHTT workings on both the Welsh and Anglia routes.

From 2006, more duties were gained by DRS, these including Class 66/4s on a circular working from Inverness that took in Aberdeen, Dundee and Perth, while further examples were based at Willesden to work the southern end of the West Coast Main Line. The year also saw the Class 20/3s deployed on the circuits from York, one duty covering much of West Yorkshire while the other traversed large chunks of south and east Yorkshire and onwards into north Lincolnshire.

RHTT operations in East Anglia saw developments on the motive power front from October 2007, this including the first use of DRS' newly acquired Class 57/0s. Equally notable was the employment of 37601 and 37603, the pair of ex Eurostar Type 3s being so new to the DRS fleet that they still carried two-tone grey. At the London end of the Great Western Main Line, DRS Class 66/4s presented an unusual sight operating a RHTT off Reading for the season.

For 2008, there was little change in DRS' RHTT circuits or motive power deployment, although more '57/0s' were drafted into East Anglia as were RETB-fitted Class 37/0s to allow the East Suffolk line to be treated. 2009 was a poor year for DRS on the RHTTs with DB Schenker taking the bulk of the work, the only remaining duties being in East Anglia and from Kingmoor to Teesside and around Cumbria and Lancashire. The motive power was still diverse though with Stowmarket hosting Class 20/3s, 37s, 57/0s and 66/4s while workings from Kingmoor typically employed English Electric or General Motors traction. The following year was much the same story but with most of DRS' active Class 20/3s tied up with London Underground stock movements, the Type 1s saw little RHTT use as did the Class 47s.

Unseasonal work

Late May 2011 brought the highly unusual sight of a water jetting RHTT at work in the spring, this having been hastily scrambled to the lowlands of Scotland form York following very strong winds that brought down considerable quantities of leaves, causing adhesion issues. This spent four days working off Grangemouth, ranging as far as Perth, Fife, Ayr, Dumbarton and Largs powered by the DRS duo of 37601 and 37611. The autumn campaign was unremarkable once again though with Class 37s and 57s working in East Anglia with both types featuring on the Kingmoor circuits alongside Class 66s.

With DB Schenker's travails in resourcing the York-based RHTT circuits, it was no surprise that DRS took the work back for 2012 with Class 20/3s once again in charge, the operational fleet having been boosted by the return of the quartet that had been on hire to GBRf. There was also change in Anglia as Class 57s achieved total motive power dominance. This included not only DRS' own Class 57s but also three of Network Rail's underutilised yellow

Modelling BR: Engineers Wagons of Privatisation 111

The war on leaves

ABOVE: GB Railfreight now largely retains its unmodified Class 73s for seasonal work, these seeing use on the Railhead Treatment Trains during the autumn and then the Snow and Ice Treatment Trains (SITT) in the winter. On October 6, 2021, 73141 *Charlotte* leads the 3W90 02.58 Tonbridge West Yard-Tonbridge West Yard circuit through Norbury Park in Surrey with 73128 *OVS Bulleid CBE* on the rear. The set is formed of two former 'binliner' KFAs configured for water jetting only. Mark Few

examples in the shape of 57305/06/10. The 2013 season saw the Class 20/3s retain their dominance in Yorkshire with the usual mix of Class 37s, 47s and 66s out of Kingmoor while the Anglia jobs were all covered by DRS-owned machines in the form of '47s' and '57s'.

There was no great change on any of the DRS circuits during 2014 or 2015, although one notable occurrence in 2015 was DRS using 66548 on northwest RHTT duties for a while, the GM being on loan from Freightliner while collision-damaged 66428 was repaired. The 2016 campaign was not a good one for the few remaining Class 20/3s as with the locos now retained solely for RHTT work and stored for the rest of the year, reliability was poor. As a result, Class 37s were called in to assist while Class 68s were even drafted onto the workings for the first time. As a result, the York-based diagrams were often rearranged at short notice or cut short to take into account the restrictions on the heavier locos.

The following year saw the English Electric Type 1s enjoy better availability but '66s' and '68s' were still on hand to assist when needed. Meanwhile, the Kingmoor and Anglia workings continued as ever during 2016 and 2017 with Class 66s evident in both areas and supported by '37s' in the north and both '37s' and '57s' in the east.

Chopper demise

2018 was another difficult year for the Class 20/3s on the York-based RHTTs following a further bout of unreliability. Just three examples were returned to service this time in the form of 20302/03/05, all playing up at some point. As a result, 20007 and 20189 were hired in from Michael Owen while Class 66s assisted as well. Meanwhile with a number of Class 37/4s now carrying BR large logo blue, there was a new livery combination to photograph, particularly on Kingmoor-based workings.

Time was finally called on the three remaining Class 20/3s following the 2019 RHTT season, during which they were often supplemented on their Yorkshire perambulations by the HNRC orange duo of 20311 and 20314. Harry Needle again provided Type 1s to DRS for 2020 but this time, the Railfreight Red stripe pairing of 20118 and 20132 shouldered much of the work as their orange sisters succumbed to reliability issues. This proved to be the last year that DRS utilised any Class 20s on its RHTTs though.

With the decline of DRS' Class 37 fleet in recent years, the Class 68s have consequently stepped up to fill the gap on RHTT duties since 2020, seeing varying use on the northwest, northeast, Yorkshire and Anglia diagrams alongside the remaining colourful Type 3s as well as Class 57s and Class 66s. Even the Class 88s have seen use, particularly working from Kingmoor but

ABOVE: With its refuse carrying days behind it, former Avon 'binliner' KFA 99 70 9310 012-8 is now employed as a RHTT flat. On December 12, 2014, the RHTT campaign was almost over for another year, but its jetting and generator module was still in need of maintenance at Tonbridge West Yard. Simon Bendall

The war on leaves

also Stowmarket, with some diagrams noted running under electric power on the West Coast and Great Eastern.

GBRf operations

GB Railfreight's involvement with RHTT workings was initially rather brief, operating just one diagram over former Great Northern metals in 2005/06, which switched to EWS operation from 2007. It was not until 2012 that the company again took on RHTT work, Peterborough once more being the operating base for circuits that covered the Great Northern route into London and also parts of the East Midlands and the east of England, all utilising Class 66/7s. These workings would return to DB Schenker operation in 2013 though.

For the 2013 season, GBRf instead commenced operation of the West Anglia RHTTs from the tamper sidings at Broxbourne, these workings running to Cambridge and also covering the c2c network and North London Line. For the initial weeks of operation in October, motive power for the two trains was provided by Network Rail Class 57/3s with 57305/06/10/12 all employed. However, the noise of the locos when laying over at Broxbourne soon led to complaints from adjacent residents, leading to Class 66s been hired in from Freightliner as replacements from the start of November until the end of the season, these being 66523/35/57 and 66621.

GBRf has continued to cover the West Anglia and c2c lines from Broxbourne since 2014, employing its ever growing Class 66/7 fleet in their many colourful liveries. More work under the wires, this time on the southern section of the West Coast, was acquired from 2019, operating from Kings Norton depot on the southern edge of Birmingham.

Southern RHTTs

For the decade or so prior to 2013, all water jetting and sandite duties on the Southern Region were carried out by Network Rail's MPV fleet. However, given the density of lines needing to be treated each day, there were not enough of the Windhoff-built vehicles to go around, leading to some routes regularly suffering from adhesion problems. As a result, that autumn saw loco-hauled RHTTs introduced on an initially small scale basis. Based at Tonbridge West Yard, their sphere of operation took in all of Kent along with some routes in Sussex and Surrey.

With the FEA wagon fleet already committed, extra wagons were needed for the Southern duties, these coming in the form of the KFA container flats previously employed on the Avon 'binliner' workings that had ceased in 2011. Given an overhaul by Network Rail as well as the new RIV numbers of 99 70 9310 001-12, these flats were of traditional skeletal construction with a full width deck rather than the central 'spine' design of the FEAs. For 2013, only four of the wagons were available and these did not enter service until that November for a rather truncated season, but subsequently all 12 have been dedicated to the southeast.

Since the introduction of the Southern RHTTs, motive power has been provided exclusively by GB Railfreight in the form of Class 66s and Class 73s along with the occasional use of hired in traction, such as Network Rail Class 57/3s for 2013 only or Class 20s from Harry Needle and Michael Owen. For the 2022 season, the newly-converted Class 69s also played a major part.

Colas operations

October 2007 saw Colas launch its operations by taking over the West Country RHTT from EWS. Operating from Par, the workings employed 47727 and 47749, which had only been released from overhaul at Eastleigh Works the previous month. Unusually, the duty was only booked for one of the Brush machines with run rounds taking place at each end of the diagram but, on occasions, both locos were deployed in top and tail form. The duo repeated the workings for a second and final year in the autumn of 2008, this including covering some branches such as Falmouth and Paignton.

Colas returned to RHTT work from the autumn of 2014, operating a single set from Kings Norton. Powered by the then recently

ABOVE: The demands placed on locos during the RHTT season are considerable with near round the clock operation, so it is no surprise that resources can be stretched, leading to hire-ins from other companies. During the 2022 campaign, 37668 saw use with both DRS and Colas and on October 21 it was recorded at Westbury standing in for a Colas Class 66 with 66850 *David Maidment OBE* on the rear. The 3S59 21.00 Swindon-Hereford circuit would run through the night, covering the Bristol area and parts of South Wales. Mark Few

The war on leaves

ABOVE: The Freightliner-operated Chiltern RHTT is one of the few examples of a three wagon set, the sandite and water jetting combination featuring six water tanks alongside the two sandite modules and jetting/generator unit. On October 6, 2021, 66519 leads 66510 through Stoke Mandeville with the 3J04 09.07 Aylesbury-Banbury on the leg to London Marylebone. As this traverses the Metropolitan Line between Amersham and Harrow-on-the-Hill, both locos are fitted with tripcocks on the bogies. Bill Atkinson

reinstated duo of 37175 and 37219, the diagrams covered an area including Bromsgrove, Worcester, Swindon and Oxford. For 2015, Colas repeated its RHTT perambulations around the Cotswolds with 47727 and 47739 undertaking the duties for much of the season, although a pair of Class 56s, 56087 and 56113, took over for the final week.

The big change for the 2016 season was Colas taking on the mid/north Wales RHTT with the small depot at Shrewsbury Coleham as the operating base. While Network Rail's Class 97/3s still performed on the Cambrian Line as far as Machynlleth, upon their return to Shrewsbury a pair of Colas '56s' would take over for the run to Holyhead and back. With this duty being one of the longest, a three wagon sandite RHTT was typically deployed but on occasions a two vehicle set was noted without the additional water-carrying FEA.

Colas also retained the Cotswold RHTT for 2016 but with a change of base to Gloucester Horton Road and with a pair of Class 56s rostered. Unfortunately, the reliability of the locos was not great, this culminating in early November with a series of failures, including that of emergency cover 56104 from UK Rail Leasing. At Network Rail's insistence, replacement motive power was hired in from Freightliner with a pair of Class 66s remaining in charge until December. Following the issues the previous year, the Cotswold RHTT spent much of the autumn of 2017 in the hands of Colas Class 66s although the company's '56s' did reappear at the end.

MML goes orange

For 2018 only, Colas expanded its RHTT commitments by taking on the Midland Main Line circuit between Toton and West Hampstead in North London, this also visiting the Leicester-Nuneaton route. In a welcome change of scene, the company's pair of Class 67s undertook the bulk of the work but when 67023 and 67027 were required for a test train outing in late November, two Class 70s were surprisingly drafted in for a few days instead. Also operated that year to assist DB was a second Colas-powered RHTT from Toton, this covering Stoke, Crewe, Worksop, Lincoln, Nottingham and Grantham during the day with an overnight leg to Derby, Matlock, Kettering, Nottingham and Newark, all worked by Class 56s.

With considerable demand on the Colas 'Grids', the locos were not always available to replace Network Rail's Class 97/3s for the trip from Shrewsbury to Holyhead with the increasingly tired-looking yellow Type 3s undertaking the whole circuit instead when needed. A pair of '56s' was in place for the final working of the year though on December 8 when Boden Rail's 50050 topped the working from Crewe for, seemingly, no particular reason.

For the Cotswold workings in 2018, the 'Grids' also needed assistance at times from fellow orange and yellow Class 66s and Class 70s, giving rise to unusual mixed class pairings. Another new RHTT working for Colas that year was from Bristol Barton Hill, taking over from DB Cargo. Typically powered by Colas '66s', there were again occasions where motive power was tight, leading to a DB-owned classmate lending a hand. The 18-hour overnight working was certainly lengthy, encompassing Westbury, Swindon, Kemble, Cardiff, assorted Welsh Valleys and the Marches route.

Today, Colas focuses its RHTT work on the mid-north Wales circuit as before and around the Cotswolds and Malverns, most recently from an operating base at Swindon. For 2022, the latter workings largely employed the company's Class 56s and Class 66s but with the use of a hired-in Class 37 from West Coast Railways at times of poor availability.

Freightliner operations

A considerable surprise for 2018 was the debut of Freightliner on RHTT workings, the company having previously had no direct involvement in the autumn campaign beyond hiring out Class 66s to Colas and GBRf when required. The choice of circuit was also interesting, being the one initially based at Acton Yard for covering the Chiltern Line.

As a result, four GMs needed to be fitted with tripcocks at Leeds Midland Road before they could be employed over the Metropolitan Line, 66510 and 66522 being the first pair completed and followed soon afterwards by 66507 and 66519. As well as running between Marylebone and Aylesbury, the main line to High Wycombe was also part of the itinerary. Freightliner still holds the route today but now employs Kings Norton as the operating base.

During mid-2020, eight of Freightliner's FRA container flats were modified at Eastleigh Works for use on RHTT duties, these receiving the necessary through wiring. Hired to Network Rail to provide additional resources, they were available in time for that autumn with a further four conversions following in the spring of 2021. Classified as FRA-B and numbered 613101-12, they have largely featured on DB-operated circuits, such as from Toton and Didcot.

ABOVE: The release of Hattons' RHTT sets in 2019 provided an easy RTR solution in OO gauge, the previous option having been the etched and resin kits from S Kits. The retailer offered both water jetting and sandite options with either a pristine or weathered finish along with an additional water tanker FEA to allow three wagon formations to be created. In contrast, N gauge has yet to see a RTR model, but various 3D-printed options are available, including from Shapeways.

114 www.keymodelworld.com